The
Most
Incredible
Cardboard
Toys in the
Whole Wide
World

LARK BOOKS

Asheville, North Carolina

The Most Incredible Cardboard Toys in the Whole Wide World

Stefan Czernecki
with Michael Haijtink

Editor: Bobbe Needham
Art Director: Celia Naranjo
Photographer: Evan Bracken
Editorial Assistants: Heather Smith and Catharine Sutherland
Production Assistants: Hannes Charen and Catharine Sutherland
Proofreader: Val Anderson

CREDITS:
A big thanks to the incredible kids in this book:
David Cobb, McKenzie Cobb, Dru Galloway, Jacob Katz,
Jasmine McAdams, Corrina Matthews, DeShawn Thurman,
Shalanda Thurman, Anna Weshner-Dunning, Tobie Weshner

Library of Congress Cataloging-in-Publication Data
Czernicki, Stefan,
    The most incredible cardboard toys in the whole wide world /
Stefan Czernecki, with Michael Haijtink.
        p. cm.
    Includes index.
    ISBN 1-57990-161-1
    1. Paper toy making. 2. Paperboard. I. Haijtink, Mic
II. Title.
TT174.5P3C94 1999
745.592—dc21

10 9 8 7 6 5 4 3 2 1
First Edition

Published by Lark Books
50 College St.
Asheville, NC 28801, USA

For information about distribution in the U.S., Canada,
the U.K., Europe,and Asia, call Lark Books at
828-253-0467.

Distributed in Australia by Capricorn Link (Australia)
  Pty Ltd., P.O. Box 6651, Baulkham Hills Business
Centre,
  NSW 2153, Australia

Distributed in New Zealand by Southern Publishers
  Group, 22 Burleigh St., Grafton,
  Auckland, New Zealand

Printed in China by Donnelley Bright Sun Printing Comp

ISBN 1-57990-161-1

Contents

Introduction   6
Toy-Making Materials, Tools, and Techniques   7

North America   11
  Mexico: Aztec Butterfly   12
  U.S.A.: Whirligigs   18
  Canada: Rodeo Rabbit   27

South America   34
  Peru: Condor Airplane   35
  Venezuela: Snake-Neck Turtle   42
  Brazil: Rio Rattles   48

Europe   54
  Italy: Donato's Dragon   55
  Spain: Pablo the Bull   62

Africa   67
  Ethiopia: Three-Toed Ostrich   68
  Congo: Congophone   73

Asia   81
  China: Yan Shih's Puppet Theater   82
  India: Darjeeling Toy Train   92
  Indonesia: Hornbill Outrigger   103

Oceania   110
  Solomon Islands: Hammerhead Sharkmobile   111
  Australia: Dreamtime Animals — Kangaroos, Honey Ant, and Rainbow Snake   117

Metric Conversion Chart   128
Index   128

Introduction

For centuries, in every corner of the world, toy makers, like other folk artists, have passed along the secrets of materials, design, and technique to their children, apprentices, and other artists. And decade upon decade, the ingenious workings, color, and entertainment of handmade toys endear them to children, and intrigue and fascinate adults.

With *The Most Incredible Cardboard Toys in the Whole Wide World*, we are passing along to you some of our own designs, so that you and the children you know can participate in this wonderful tradition and become toy makers yourselves. We believe that handmade toys speak to the child in all of us.

Handmade toys differ in many respects from mass-produced toys. Every toy is unique, and each toy reflects the personality of its maker. The toys you create from the patterns in this book won't look exactly like ours, because you will add your own touches and modify the designs to your own taste. You may find that some of the toys we've designed work best as decorative art for a child's room (or any room). We intend them to be the kind of toys that are cherished and treated with the care you would encourage a child to show any precious possession.

In designing the toys in this book, we found inspiration in folk toys, art, and stories from around the world—from Darjeeling to Rio, the Solomon Islands to the Congo. Among the toys you'll find a Condor Airplane from Peru, a Rodeo Rabbit from Canada, and a Three-Toed Ostrich from Ethiopia. For every one, we've written a tale about that toy to share with children.

Folk-toy makers create toys with simple tools, from whatever materials are plentiful and cheap—for example, clay, straw, tin, wood, and paper. For the toys in this book, we have used inexpensive materials such as cardboard, cardboard tubes, wooden dowels and washers, corrugated paper, paint, and glue. Our tools were a handsaw, a drill, a knife, and scissors.

You may want to start right in with one of the toys in the book, or you may want to find inspiration on your own first and adapt a pattern to your own design. Before you begin, you may want to read a book of folk tales from a land that especially intrigues you, or look at examples of art from around the world. You might choose to wander through a zoo to get in the toy-making mood, or you might visit the creatures in an aquarium.

There are no rules in the world of handmade toys and toy making. However you decide to enter that realm, you'll find great scope for inventiveness and imagination, enjoyment in the making, and pleasure in your own one-of-a-kind toys.

Toy-Making Materials, Tools, and Techniques

MATERIALS AND TOOLS

▶ For each toy in the book, you will find a list of materials, but you will use the same basic materials for all of them.

Two-ply cardboard	Corrugated paper
Cardboard tubes	Acrylic paint
Wooden dowels	Wood glue
Sandpaper	Tracing paper
Clips and rubber bands	White acrylic gesso

▶ For some toys you will need:

String	Wooden eggs
Wood pieces	Ribbons, pom-poms, pipe cleaners, felt
Wooden washers	

▶ Most materials are available at art-supply stores or craft stores; some of these stores carry corrugated paper in various colors. Some items, such as wooden dowels and washers, you will find at hardware stores.

▶ You will need some simple tools:

Pencil   Handsaw

Steel ruler   Electric hand drill

Craft knife   Paintbrushes

Scissors

GENERAL DIRECTIONS FOR ALL THE TOYS

You'll find the instructions for each toy color-coded to the drawings and figures that accompany it. The photographs show how we chose to paint and decorate each toy, but you will probably choose different colors and detailing. A metric conversion table appears on page 128.

Selecting and Fitting Cardboard Tubes

▶ All the toys call for one or more cardboard tubes of various sizes, with diameters of from 1 inch (2.5 cm) to 5¼ inches (13.1 cm). Tubes at least ⅛ inch (.3 cm) thick make sturdy toys.

▶ Most of the toys require a tube ⅛ inch (.3 cm) thick and 3¼ inches (8.1 cm) in diameter. This tube is available in a standard size: 3¼ x 33 inches (8.1 x 82.5 cm).

▶ To fit two tubes together: When you need to shape one end of a tube to fit the curve of a second tube (for instance, the neck and head of Rodeo Rabbit in the photo), tape a piece of sand-

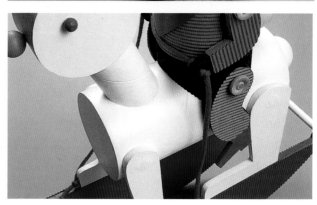

For Rodeo Rabbit, you need to fit a tube 1¾ inches (4.4 cm) in diameter (the neck) snugly against a tube 3¼ inches (8.1 cm) in diameter (the head). First, tape sandpaper around a tube the size of the head tube. Sand one end of the neck tube against the sandpaper until you shape it to the curve of the head tube. The neck is then ready to be glued to the actual head tube. (Keep the sandpaper-covered tube; you may be able to use it again.)

paper around a third tube with the same diameter as the second. Then sand the end of the first tube against it.

Using Two-Ply Cardboard

▶ You will use two-ply (two-layer) cardboard to make all the toys. Often the directions call for two or three layers of two-ply cardboard for extra strength. For example, to make a six-ply wheel, you will cut three circles from two-ply cardboard and glue them together.

(The directions for each toy indicate the number of plies to use for each piece.

Two ply	=	one sheet	=	$3/32$ inch (.25 cm)
Four ply	=	two sheets	=	$3/16$ inch (.5 cm)
Six ply	=	three sheets	=	$1/4$ inch (.6 cm)
Eight ply	=	four sheets	=	$3/8$ inch (.9 cm)
Ten ply	=	five sheets	=	$15/32$ inch (1.25 cm)

▶ Use clips and rubber bands to hold several glued pieces of two-ply cardboard together. When the glue is dry, sand the edges for a perfect fit.

Cutting and Drilling

▶ Cut cardboard pieces and slits in tubes with a craft knife.
▶ Drill holes with an electric hand drill. Depending on the toy, you may need drill bits measuring $13/64$ and $3/16$ inch (.5 cm), $1/4$ inch (.6 cm), $5/16$ inch (.8 cm), and $3/8$ inch (.9 cm).

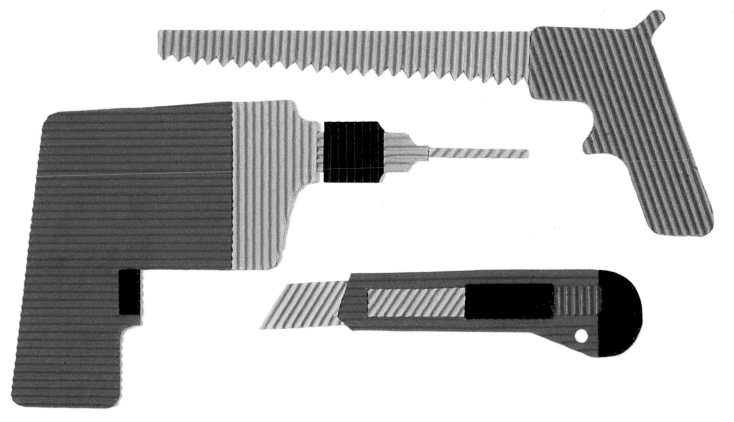

Sanding and Adjusting

▶ For a perfect fit between cardboard pieces and dowels and the slits and holes in the tubes, you can expect to do some sanding and adjusting.

▶ Use different grades of sandpaper to smooth surfaces and adjust slits, moving from coarse to fine as needed. Wear a dust mask when sanding.

Gluing

▶ Use wood glue for all the toys.

Painting and Corrugating

▶ Before painting a toy, paint the pieces of cardboard and the tubes with white acrylic gesso, available from art and craft departments and art-supply stores.

▶ When the gesso is dry, sand the surfaces with fine sandpaper, then paint the pieces with acrylic paints.

▶ After the paint on the tubes and cardboard pieces has dried, you will cover many parts of the toys with corrugated paper.

▶ In the step labeled "painting and corrugating" in the instructions for each toy, the process of corrugating includes these steps:

1. Measure and cut out the corrugated paper you will need to cover each piece. If the corrugated paper you are using is not predyed, paint your brown corrugated paper with white acrylic gesso.

2. When the gesso is dry, paint the paper with acrylic paint in the desired color.

3. On tracing paper, trace the slits and holes in the pieces to be corrugated, then transfer the markings to the smooth side of the corrugated paper.

4. Cut out the slits and holes in the corrugated paper, then glue the paper onto the tube. Hold the paper in place with rubber bands until the glue has dried.

NORTH AMERICA

Mexico

Aztec Butterfly

Princess Mayahuel's Friend

Even though Mayahuel was an Aztec princess, she was lonely, for no other children lived in the palace, and she had no one to play with.

Her only friend was a redspotted yellow orchid on a hanging vine in the royal garden.

Every day when she watered the vine, she said, "Oh, little orchid! Where will I ever find someone to play with?"

And every day the orchid drooped a little as it watched Mayahuel dance alone in the royal garden or sit sadly alone on a bench. The princess never laughed or even smiled.

"She takes such good care of me," thought the little orchid. "There must be something I can do to cheer her up."

One early summer day, the orchid had an idea. "Xochiquetzal, great goddess of flowers," she begged. "Can you transform me into a flying flower, so I can dance and play with Princess Mayahuel and make her happy?" That night, Xochiquetzal changed the orchid into a bright butterfly with yellow and red spots.

When Mayahuel came to water the orchid the next morning, she found a dancing butterfly instead. All day the red and yellow butterfly and Mayahuel celebrated. They danced through the garden and played tag and hide and seek, which the butterfly never won because it couldn't stay still long enough. Mayahuel smiled and laughed and giggled all day. At last she had found a friend.

Tale Tidbits

• A Native American people, the Aztecs ruled a mighty empire in Mexico during the 1400s and early 1500s.

• The butterfly was a common symbol for Xochiquetzal, the Aztec goddess of flowers and beauty.

• The Aztecs associated butterflies with transformation, because of their progress from caterpillar to cocooned pupa to butterfly.

• The Aztec Butterfly takes its inspiration from early Aztec stone carvings and masks and from Mexican folk toys.

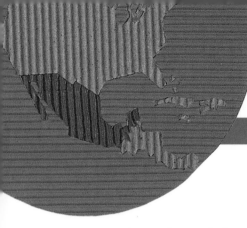

How to Make an Aztec Butterfly

MATERIALS

- Cardboard tubes, 1¼, 1¾, 3¼, and 5¼ inches in diameter
- 2-ply cardboard
- Clips and rubber bands
- Wood glue
- Wooden dowels, ³⁄₁₆, ¼, and ⅜ inch in diameter
- Fine, medium, and coarse sandpaper
- 2 wooden balls, ⅜ inch in diameter
- Wooden ball, ⅞ inch in diameter
- Acrylic white gesso
- Acrylic paint in desired colors
- Tracing paper
- Corrugated paper

TOOLS

- Pencil
- Steel ruler
- Cutting knife
- Scissors
- Handsaw
- Electric hand drill with ³⁄₁₆, ¼, and ⅜-inch bits

Before you begin: Be sure to read the General Instructions, pages 8–10.

HATCHING THE BUTTERFLY
BODY (BLUE)

1. Cut a 12-inch piece of 3¼-inch tube.
2. Cut two ¾ x 3inch slits in the top, 4 inches from the front edge.
3. Drill two ¼-inch holes in the top of the tube and one ⅜-inch hole in the bottomcenter of the tube.
4. Cut a round 4-ply lid 3¼ inches in diameter, and glue it on to close the back end of the tube.

FLYING MECHANISM (GREEN)

1. Cut a 1 x 3-inch piece of 10-ply cardboard.
2. With sandpaper, shape the 1-inch ends to fit the inside curve of the tube.
3. Drill a ⅜-inch hole in the bottom center of the cardboard, ¼-inch deep, and drill two ¼-inch holes in the top, ¼-inch deep.
4. Cut two 1¾-inch pieces of ¼-inch dowel, and round off one end of each.
5. Glue the dowels into the holes in the cardboard (see fig. 1).
6. Cut an 8-inch piece of ⅜-inch dowel.
7. Drill a ⅜-inch hole in the ⅞-inch wooden ball, and glue the dowel into the ball for the pulling stick.

WINGS (RED)

1. Cut two wings with attached hinges from 4-ply cardboard.
2. On the underside of each wing, build up the hinge to 8-ply; drill a generous ³⁄₁₆-inch hole so that a ³⁄₁₆-inch dowel will fit into it loosely (see fig. 2).

HEAD (ORANGE)

1. Cut a 1-inch piece of 5¼-inch tube.
2. Cut two ¼ x ¾-inch slits for the ears, and drill two ³⁄₁₆-inch holes for the antennas.
3. Cut two round 5¼-inch lids from 4-ply card-board.
4. In one lid, cut a ¼ x 1-inch slit for the nose and two 1½-inch slits for the eyes.
5. Glue on the lids to close up the head tube, with slits to the front.

EARS, MOUTH, EYEBROWS, PROBOSCIS, AND ANTENNAS (PURPLE)

1. Cut two ears from 6-ply cardboard.
2. For the mouth, cut a 1-inch piece of 1¼-inch tube.
3. Cut a ½-inch piece of 1¾-inch tube, then cut the piece into two 1½-inch eyebrows.
4. Cut the proboscis (a sucking tube) from 6-ply cardboard.
5. For the antennas, cut two 6½-inch pieces of ³⁄₁₆-inch dowel.
6. Drill a ³⁄₁₆-inch hole in each ⅜-inch wooden ball, and glue the dowels into them.

PAINTING AND CORRUGATING

1. Paint the front and back lids of the head except where the body will be glued. Corrugate the edge of the head.
2. Paint the fronts and edges of the ears. Corrugate the backs of the ears except for the bottoms, which will be inserted into the head.
3. Paint the eyebrows, proboscis, mouth, and antennas.
4. Corrugate the body.
5. Paint the edges of the wings and hinges. Corrugate both sides of the wings except the hinges. On the bottom of the wings, leave clear an area ½ x 1½ inches from the center of the hinges.

ASSEMBLING

1. On the head, glue, in this order: the ears in the ear slits, the proboscis in its slit, the eyebrows and mouth on the face, the antennas in the holes.
2. Place the 10-ply flying-mechanism piece in the body, and line up the ¼-inch dowels with the ¼-inch holes in the body, then push them through the holes.
3. Slide the ⅜-inch pulling-stick dowel through the hole in the body and glue it in the bottom center hole in the flying-mechanism piece (see fig. 3).
4. Cut a 10-inch piece of ³⁄₁₆-inch dowel.
5. Slide the wing hinges into the slits in the body and interlock them (see fig. 4). Then slide the 10-inch-long dowel through the hinges, leaving the dowel "floating" free lengthwise in the body tube (see fig. 4).
6. Glue the head to the body.

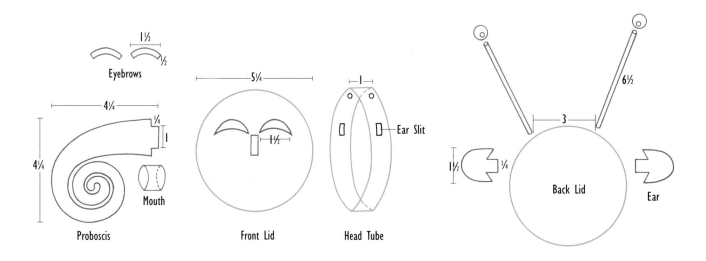

Eyebrows 1½ ½

Proboscis 4¼ 4¼ ¼ Mouth

Front Lid 5¼ 1½

Head Tube 1 Ear Slit

Back Lid 6½ 3 1½ ¾ Ear

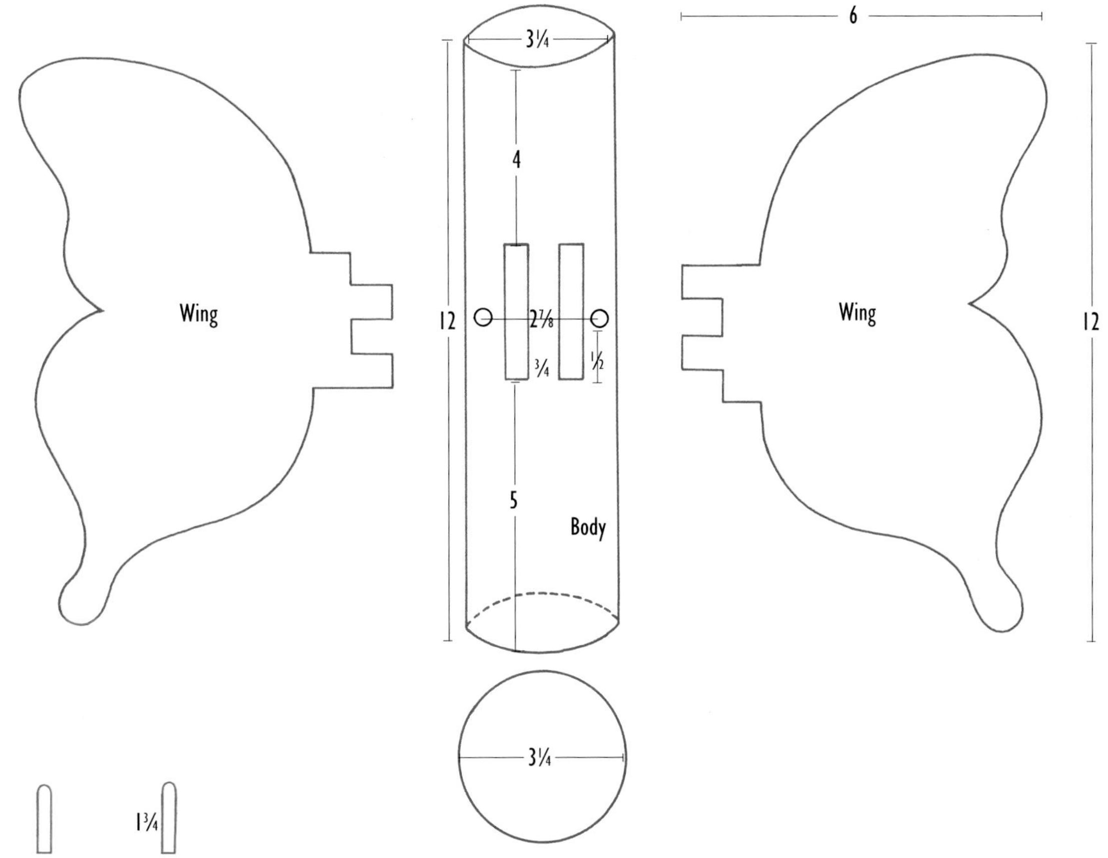
3¼
6
4
Wing
12
2⅞
¾
½
5
Body
Wing
12
3¼

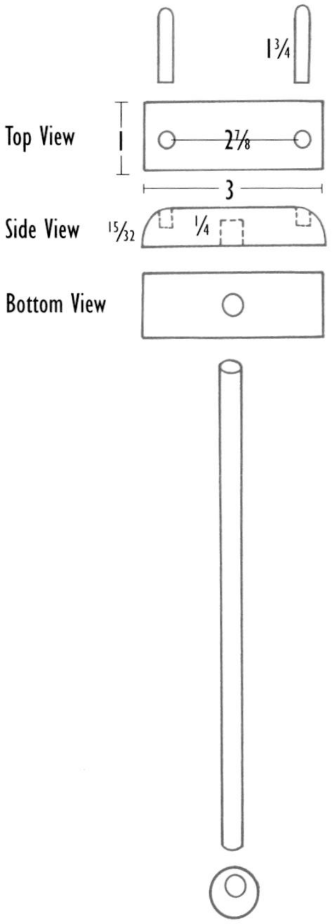
1¾
Top View
1
2⅞
3
Side View
15/32
¼
Bottom View

FIGURE 1. Creating the flying mechanism

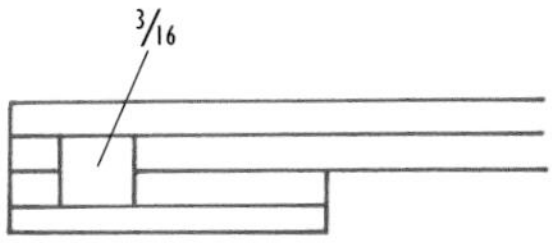
3/16

FIGURE 2. 8-ply hinge, top view

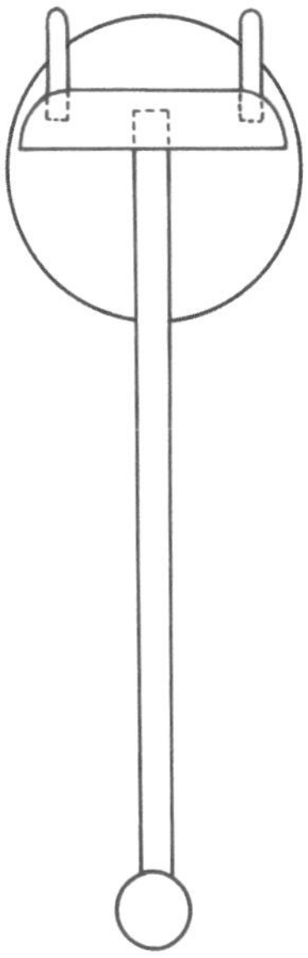

FIGURE 3

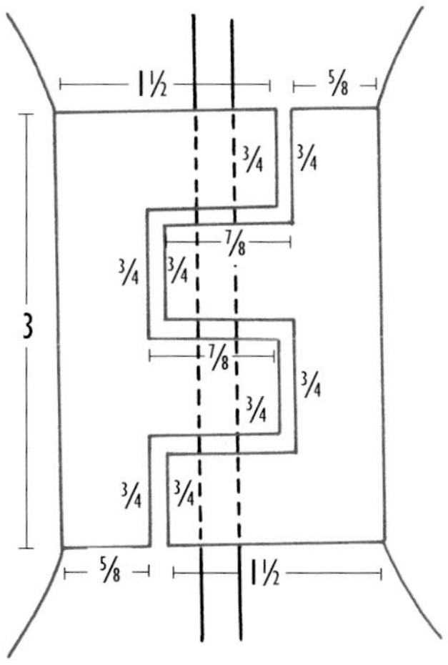
1½
⅝
¾
¾
⅞
¾
¾
3
⅞
¾
¾
¾
¾
⅝
1½

FIGURE 4. Hinges

United States of America

Whirligigs

The Whirligigs and the Declaration of Independence

In the small town of Plymouth, Pennsylvania, July of 1776 was especially hot. All the Plymouth farmers could talk about was how the heat made their animals sick, made their friends cranky, and made their children beg to go swimming in the creek every hour of the day.

Cornelius was a Plymouth chicken farmer, and at the market one early July morning he was complaining about the heat like everyone else. No one wanted to buy his eggs.

"It's too hot to cook them," said one person after another.

As he sat staring at his unsold eggs, through the dusty heat of the market came a shout. "Have you heard? Have you heard?" people were asking each other.

"What?" Cornelius wanted to know. "Have I heard what?" He hoped it wasn't anything about the heat.

Another farmer called out to him, "The Declaration's finally finished! Everyone's signed! We're going to Philadelphia to celebrate!" The colonies had been at war with England for more than a year. Now at last the Congress had adopted the final draft of their Declaration of Independence.

Independence! Cornelius thought. He forgot all about no one buying his eggs.

Philadelphia wasn't far away, he thought. He forgot all about his eggs entirely. I want to make something special to celebrate the event, he decided.

At home in his workshop, he even forgot all about the heat. He began throwing pieces of wood around. "Not this one, not this," he muttered. "Just right. I want it just right." Finally he found some wood that satisfied him, and he started to carve. He wanted something exciting. Something funny. Something about independence, and something about chickens. And of course, something red, white, and blue, the colors of America's first national flag.

Something that could whirl and twirl in the wind, like the flag, Cornelius thought, as he carved and cut and glued.

Many days later, as he walked down the street in front of the Pennsylvania State House, Cornelius carried his finished inventions. He called them whirligigs. As he passed, children and grownups stopped and stared and then laughed as the red, white, and blue whirligigs whirled and twirled in the wind, celebrating American independence.

Tale Tidbits

▶ The word *whirligig* is a combination of *whirl* and *gig*, meaning a top. The word dates back to 1570—*whyrl-egyge*, in Middle English.

▶ Whirligigs were first mentioned in U.S. literature in Washington Irving's "The Legend of Sleepy Hollow," published in 1819. All through the nineteenth century, you could drive down a country road and see whirligigs twirling in front yards and farmyards.

▶ Today whirligigs are distinctly U.S. wind toys. The design for these comes from the classic weathervane.

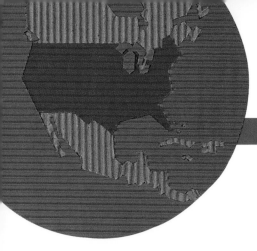

How to Make a Whirligig

MATERIALS (FOR TWO WHIRLIGIGS)

▶ Cardboard tubes, 1¼, 1½, and 3¼ inches in diameter
▶ 1-ply and 2-ply cardboard
▶ Clips and rubber bands
▶ Fine, medium, and coarse sandpaper
▶ Wood glue
▶ Acrylic white gesso
▶ Acrylic paint in desired colors
▶ Tracing paper
▶ Corrugated paper
▶ 4 wooden washers, ¾ inch in diameter
▶ Wooden dowels, ¼, ⅜, and ³⁄₁₆-inch in diameter
▶ 4 wooden washers, 1 inch in diameter

TOOLS

▶ Pencil
▶ Steel ruler
▶ Cutting knife
▶ Scissors
▶ Handsaw
▶ Electric hand drill with ³⁄₁₆, ⁵⁄₁₆, and ⅜-inch bits
▶ Paintbrushes

Before you begin: Be sure to read the General Instructions, pages 8–10.

HATCHING THE HEN OR ROOSTER

Note: The hen and the rooster are identical except for the head and tail designs.

BODY (BLUE)

1. Cut a 5-inch piece of 3¼-inch tube.
2. Cut two opposite pairs of end slits at the top and bottom of the body, each ¼ x 1½ inches.
3. Drill a ⅜-inch hole in the bottom center, two ⁵⁄₁₆-inch holes in each side center, and a ³⁄₁₆-inch hole in the top center.
4. Cut two ⅜ x 2-inch horizontal slits, 2¼ inches from the top.
5. Cut a 2 x 3 x ⅜-inch piece of 8-ply cardboard for a stick holder. Drill a ⅜-inch hole in the bottom center of this piece, ¼ inch deep (see fig. 1). (The hole should not go all the way through.)
6. Hole-side down, insert this piece through the horizontal slits, lining up the hole with the hole in the bottom of the body tube, and glue it in place. (This will help hold the stick in place later.) Sand the edges of the piece to fit the curve of the body tube.
7. Cut two round 3¼-inch lids from 4-ply cardboard. Cut a ¼-inch-wide strip out of the center of each lid, so that you end up with four half-lids, each 1½ inches across. Glue one half-lid on each side of the slits at the ends of the body, closing the tube.

WHIRLERS (RED)

1. Cut two 1¼-inch pieces of 1¼-inch tube. Shape one end of each piece to fit the curve of the body tube (see fig. 2).
2. Cut two round 1¼-inch lids from 2-ply cardboard, and drill a ⁵⁄₁₆-inch hole through the center of each. Glue on the lids to close each cylinder on one end.
3. Line up one whirler tube on each side of the body, and draw its outline on the body.
4. Draw a 1½-inch circle around the ³⁄₁₆-inch hole in the top of the body tube.
5. For the hen only: Cut out four stars from 1-ply cardboard. Trace the star shapes on the body tube.

HEAD, TAIL, AND WINGS (GREEN)

1. Cut the head and tail from 6-ply cardboard.
2. For the wings, cut two 3-inch pieces of 1¼-inch tube. In the center of each, drill a ⁵⁄₁₆-inch hole all the way through.
3. At one end of each tube, cut ³⁄₁₆ x 1-inch vertical slits opposite each other, making in each tube a ³⁄₁₆-inch slit for one wing to slide into. At the other end of each tube, cut another pair of ³⁄₁₆ x 1-inch vertical slits opposite each other, placed so that the second wing can slide in the resulting ³⁄₁₆-inch slit at right angles to the first wing.

4. Cut four round 1¼-inch lids from 2-ply cardboard. Cut a ¼-inch-wide strip out of the center of each lid, to end up with eight half-lids, each ½ inch across. Glue one half-lid on each side of the slits.
5. Cut four wings from 4-ply cardboard.

PAINTING AND CORRUGATING

1. Paint the edges of the head. Corrugate the head except for the end that will be inserted into the body. Paint two ¾-inch washers, and glue one on each side for eyes. Glue the head in the front body slit.
2. Paint the edges of the tail. Corrugate the tail except for the end that will be inserted into the body. Glue the tail in the back body slit.
3. Corrugate the body except for the areas outlined on the top and sides (and for the hen, leave the star areas uncorrugated).
4. Paint the 1¼-inch whirler tubes and the wings.
5. Paint two 1-inch washers for the whirlers.

ASSEMBLING THE HEN OR ROOSTER

1. For the hen, glue on the stars.
2. Glue the shaped 1¼-inch whirler tubes on the sides of the body in line with the ⁵⁄₁₆-inch holes.
3. Glue the wings in the slits of the 3-inch tubes (see fig. 3).
4. Cut a 9-inch piece of ¼-inch dowel, and slide it horizontally through the holes in the body and wings (lavender).
5. Leaving space between the whirler tube and the

wing tube for easy turning, glue a 1-inch wooden washer on the end of each dowel (lavender).

6. Cut a 20-inch piece of ⅜-inch dowel, slide it through the hole in the bottom of the body tube, and snug it into the hole in the anchoring piece inside the body.

MOUNTING THE SUN AND MOON RIDERS

Note: The sun and moon figures riding the hen and rooster are identical except for the heads.

BODY, ARMS, AND LEGS (ORANGE)

1. Cut a 2¾-inch piece of 1½-inch tube for the body. Shape one end of the piece to fit the curve of the hen/rooster body (see fig. 4).
2. Drill two ³⁄₁₆-inch holes for arms and two ³⁄₁₆-inch holes for legs (see fig. 4).
3. Cut a round 1½-inch lid from 2-ply cardboard, and drill a ³⁄₁₆-inch hole through its center. Glue on the lid to close the top of the tube.
4. Cut two arms and two legs from 6-ply cardboard. Drill ³⁄₁₆-inch holes through each arm and leg for joining.

SUN HEAD (PURPLE)

1. Cut a ½-inch piece from 3¼-inch tube. Drill a ³⁄₁₆-inch hole through the bottom.
2. Cut two round 3¼-inch lids from 2-ply cardboard for the head front and back.
3. Glue on the lids to close the head tube.

MOON HEAD (LIME)

1. Cut a ½-inch piece from 3¼-inch tube. Cut the piece in half.
2. Cut two 3¼-inch moon-shaped lids from 2-ply cardboard, and glue one lid to each side of the half-cylinder.
3. Cut a ½-inch strip from 1-ply cardboard, and glue it on the inside curve of the moon (see fig. 5).

PAINTING AND CORRUGATING

1. Paint the top of the body, and corrugate the body tube.
2. Paint the arms, legs, and the sun or moon head.

ASSEMBLING THE WHIRLIGIG (PINK)

1. Cut two 2½-inch pieces of ³⁄₁₆-inch dowel, slide them horizontally through the body tube, and attach the arms and legs (see fig. 6).

2. Cut a 3½-inch piece of ³⁄₁₆-inch dowel. Glue the sun or moon head on one end of the dowel, then slide the dowel through the body, leaving space between the head and body so the head can turn freely (see fig. 7).

3. Glue the sun or moon figure on the body of the hen or rooster.

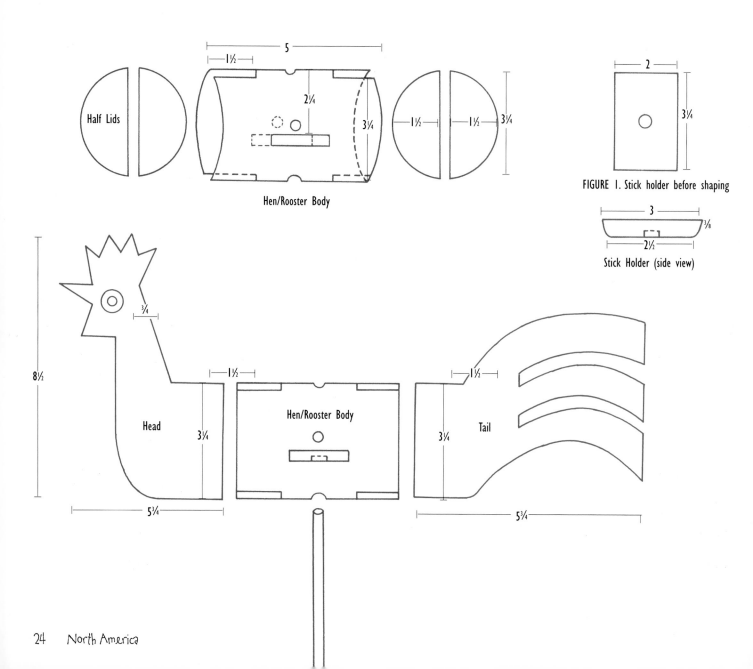

Half Lids

Hen/Rooster Body

FIGURE 1. Stick holder before shaping

Stick Holder (side view)

Head

Hen/Rooster Body

Tail

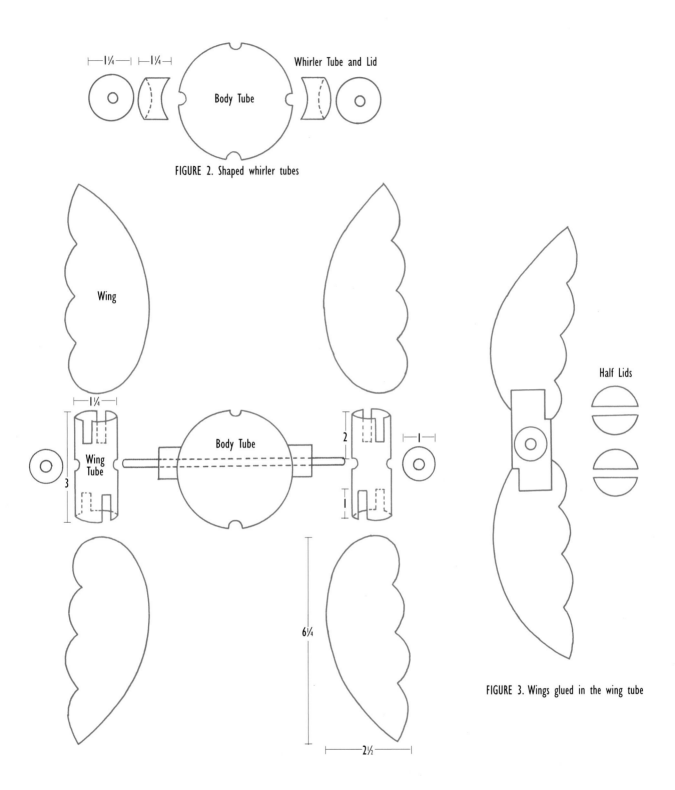

FIGURE 2. Shaped whirler tubes

Whirler Tube and Lid

Body Tube

1¼ · 1¼

Wing

1¼

Wing Tube

Body Tube

3

2

1

1

6¼

2½

Half Lids

FIGURE 3. Wings glued in the wing tube

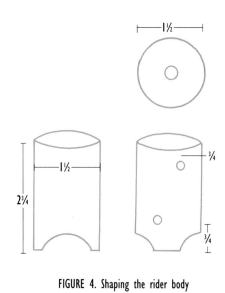

FIGURE 4. Shaping the rider body

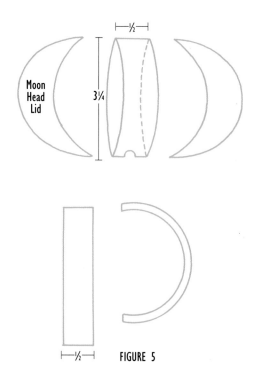

Moon
Head
Lid

½

3¼

½

FIGURE 5

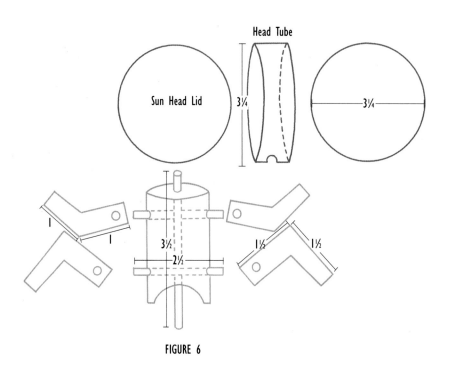

Sun Head Lid

Head Tube

3¼

3¼

3½

2½

1½   1½

1

1

FIGURE 6

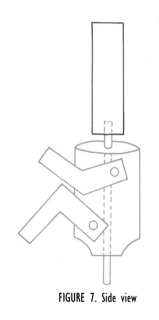

FIGURE 7. Side view

Canada

Rodeo
Rabbit

John Ware and the Snow Rabbit

One dark winter night, the snow blew across the western Canadian prairie so thick and fast you could build a snowman in the air. John Ware and five other cowboys huddled around a campfire wearing all the clothes they had and wrapped in every blanket they owned. They were keeping watch over a herd of cattle, to be sure none were buried under the snow.

All night John Ware warmed his fingers at the fire so he could play his guitar, and the cowboys took turns telling stories, trying to see who could tell the tallest tale. One cowboy told the story of the giant snow rabbit, which he said could kill a man or a cow just by looking at it.

"You're kiddin' me," said John Ware. "There ain't nothin' like that! Ah'm not scared!"

Behind him, from somewhere in the thick, driving snow, came a series of crashes as loud as thunder. The cattle panicked and ran in circles, bumping into each other, threatening to stampede into the white night.

Tale Tidbits

▶ Born on a South Carolina plantation, John Ware came to the Canadian prairies to work as a cattle hand in the 1880s. He was an expert horseman and the best bronco buster and steer wrestler on the prairies.

▶ The design for the Rodeo Rabbit is based on the traditional rocking horse and inspired by western Canadian folk art. The toy rocking horse dates back to the early 17th century.

But the cowboys stopped worrying about the cattle, because out of the blizzard leaped a giant snow rabbit. Its ears were as long as a man's body. Its pink nose was as big as a man's fist. Its legs stretched almost as high as a man's shoulder. In fact, it was as big as a horse—at least. Five of the cowboys closed their eyes and shook in their boots.

The sixth cowboy, John Ware, flung his lasso over the rabbit's neck, took a running jump and leaped onto the rabbit's back, and seized the rabbit's long ears. "All right, you big bunny!" he yelled. "Let's go!" The rabbit jumped into the air and twisted around five times, trying to throw John Ware off his back. He kicked his hind legs so hard and high he made a huge wall of snow between himself and the trembling cowboys. But John Ware held on tight.

When the cowboys peeped around the snow wall, all they could see were huge rabbit prints disappearing into the blizzard. John Ware and the rabbit were nowhere to be seen.

"Reckon the snow rabbit killed ol' John," one of the cowboys said, shaking his head. "Naw, he didn't," said another cowboy. "Don't see his body, do you? Or his footprints either. He rode that rabbit out of here, you can bet on it."

And forever afterward, when a blizzard blows so thick across the western prairie you can make a snowman in the air, someone will swear that through the driving flakes they saw a cowboy riding an enormous white rabbit through the snowy night, his guitar strapped on his back.

How to Make a Rodeo Rabbit

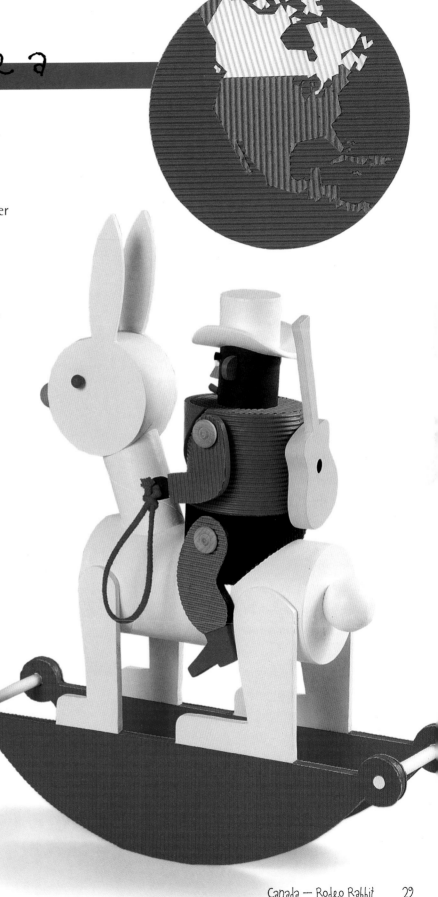

MATERIALS

- Cardboard tubes, 1¾ and 3¼ inches in diameter
- 2-ply cardboard
- Clips and rubber bands
- Wooden ball, 1½ inches in diameter
- Wooden ball, ¾-inch in diameter
- Wooden dowels, ³⁄₁₆ and ⁵⁄₁₆ inches in diameter
- Wood glue
- 1½ cups rice
- 2 tie-rack knobs
- Fine, medium, and coarse sandpaper
- Acrylic white gesso
- Acrylic paints in desired colors
- Tracing paper
- Corrugated paper
- 4 wooden washers, ¾ inch in diameter
- Colored cord for lasso

TOOLS

- Pencil
- Steel ruler
- Cutting knife
- Scissors
- Handsaw
- Electric hand drill with ³⁄₁₆, ⁵⁄₁₆, and ³⁄₈-inch bits
- Paintbrushes

Before you begin: Be sure to read the General Instructions, pages 8–10.

SADDLING UP THE RABBIT

BODY (BLUE)

1. Cut a 7-inch piece of 3¼-inch tube. Cut a 1¾-inch hole for the neck, ½ inch from one end.
2. Drill four ⁵⁄₁₆-inch holes, two on each side, ½ inch from each end, for the legs/rockers.
3. Cut two round lids from 4-ply cardboard, 3¼ inches in diameter.
4. Drill a ³⁄₁₆-inch hole through the center of one lid, and glue on the lid to close the back of the body tube. Glue the other lid to close the front of the body tube.

TAIL, HEAD, AND EARS (RED)

1. For the tail, drill a ³⁄₁₆-inch hole ½ inch deep in the 1½-inch wooden ball. Cut a 1-inch piece of ³⁄₁₆-inch dowel, and glue the dowel in the hole.
2. For the head, cut a 1½-inch piece of 3¼-inch tube. Drill a ³⁄₁₆-inch hole for the nose.
3. Cut two face/ear pieces from 4-ply cardboard. Drill a ³⁄₁₆-inch hole through the center of each piece for eyes.
4. Glue on one face/ear piece to close one side of the face tube. Fill the head with rice for extra weight, and glue the other face/ear piece to close the tube.

NOSE, EYES, NECK, AND ROCKERS (GREEN)

1. For the nose, cut a 1-inch piece of ³⁄₁₆-inch dowel. Drill a ³⁄₁₆-inch hole ¼ inch deep in the ¾ -inch wooden ball and glue the dowel into the hole.
2. Trim off part of the stems of two tie-rack knobs; the knobs will be the eyes.
3. For the neck, cut a 4-inch piece of 1¾-inch tube, and sand one end of the tube to fit the curve of the head.
4. From 2-ply cardboard, cut a 1¾-inch lid, and glue it on to close the bottom of the neck tube.
5. From 6-ply cardboard, cut two legs/rockers. Drill a ⁵⁄₁₆-inch hole in the top of each leg.

PAINTING AND CORRUGATING

1. Paint, in this order: the body, tail, head, nose, eyes, and neck.
2. Paint the legs and corrugate the base of the rockers on both sides.

ASSEMBLING THE RABBIT

1. Cut four 3¾-inch pieces of ⁵⁄₁₆-inch dowel. Slide the dowels through the holes in the body and rockers, and glue them in.
2. Glue the tail to the body, and glue the nose and eyes in the head.
3. Fill the neck with rice for extra weight. Glue the head on the neck, but do not attach the neck to the body yet.

MOUNTING THE COWBOY

BODY (ORANGE)

1. Cut a 4½-inch piece of 3¼-inch tube, and sand one end of the tube to fit the curve of the rabbit body (see fig. 1).
2. Drill a ³⁄₁₆-inch hole on each side for the arms and a ³⁄₁₆-inch hole on each side for the legs. Drill two ³⁄₁₆-inch holes on the back for the guitar.
3. Cut a round 3¼-inch lid from 4-ply cardboard, and glue on the lid to close the top of the body tube.

BANDANA, ARMS, LEGS, AND HAT (PURPLE)

1. For the bandana, cut out a 2 x 3½-inch triangle from 3¼-inch tube.
2. From 4-ply cardboard, cut two arms/hands and two legs/feet, and drill a ³⁄₁₆-inch hole in each arm/hand and upper leg.
3. For the hat, cut a 1½-inch piece of 1¾-inch tube.
4. Cut a round 1¾-inch lid from 4-ply cardboard, and glue on the lid to close the top of the hat.
5. Cut a round 2¾-inch brim from 3¼-inch tube. Sand the bottom of the hat to fit the curve of the brim, and glue the hat to the brim.

HEAD (PINK)

1. Cut a 1¾-inch piece of 1¾-inch tube, and sand the top to fit the curve of the hat.
2. Cut two ³⁄₁₆ x ¼-inch slits for the ears.
3. Cut two ears from 4-ply cardboard.
4. Cut eyes, eyebrows, nose, and mouth from 2-ply cardboard (not shown).

GUITAR (LIME)

1. Cut the guitar from 4-ply cardboard. Build up the body of the guitar to 8-ply.

2. Drill a ³⁄₈-inch hole ¼ inch deep in the center of the guitar front, and two ³⁄₁₆-inch holes ¼ inch deep in the guitar back, corresponding to the holes in the cowboy's back.
3. Cut two 1-inch pieces of ³⁄₁₆-inch dowel, and glue them into the holes in the back of the guitar.

PAINTING AND CORRUGATING

1. Corrugate the body except where the bandana will be glued. Corrugate the top of the body except where the head will be glued.
2. Paint the bandana. Paint the inside of the arms, and corrugate the outside except the hands. Paint the inside of the legs, and corrugate the outside except the boots.
3. Paint, in this order: the hat, head, ears, eyes, eyebrows, nose, mouth, and guitar.

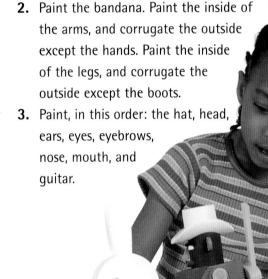

ASSEMBLING THE COWBOY

1. Glue, in this order: the bandana on the body; the ears in the head slits; the eyes, eyebrows, nose, and mouth on the face; the hat on the head; and the head on the body.
2. Cut two 4½-inch pieces of ³⁄₁₆-inch dowel. Slide one dowel through the body and the arms; leaving space between the arms and the body for free movement, attach a ¾-inch washer on each end of the dowel (see fig. 2).
3. Repeat step 2 for the legs.
4. Make a lasso from colored cord and attach it to the hands.

5. Insert the guitar dowels into the cowboy's back and glue the guitar to the back (see fig. 3).

ASSEMBLING THE RODEO RABBIT

1. Slide the rabbit's neck into the body.
2. Put the cowboy on the rabbit's back, and adjust the angle of the rabbit's neck and the placement of the cowboy until the balance is right.
3. Glue the rabbit's neck and the cowboy to the rabbit.

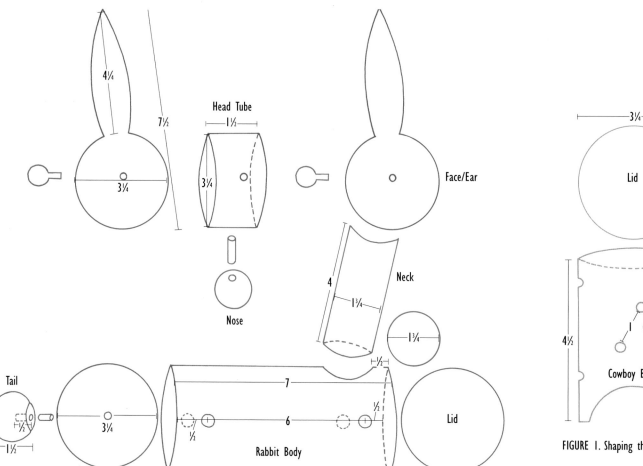

FIGURE I. Shaping the cowboy body

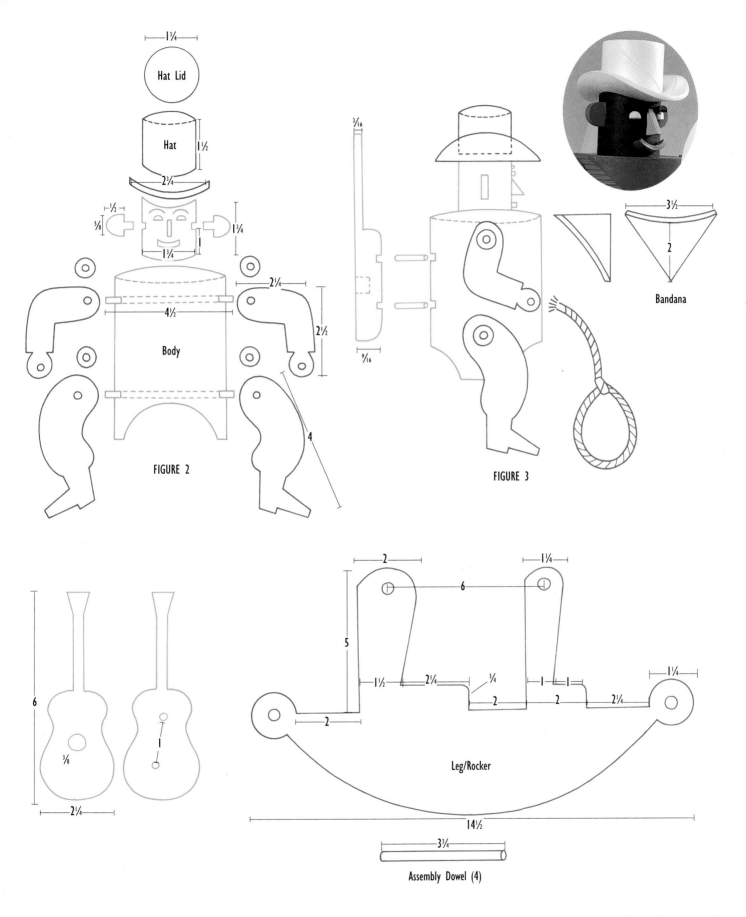

1¾

Hat Lid

Hat   1½

2¾

½   5/8   1¾   1

4½

Body

2¼   2½

4

FIGURE 2

3/16

9/16

FIGURE 3

3½

2

Bandana

6   3/8   2¼

2

5

1½   2¼   ¾   1   1   1¼

2   2   2   2¼

Leg/Rocker

14½

3¾

Assembly Dowel (4)

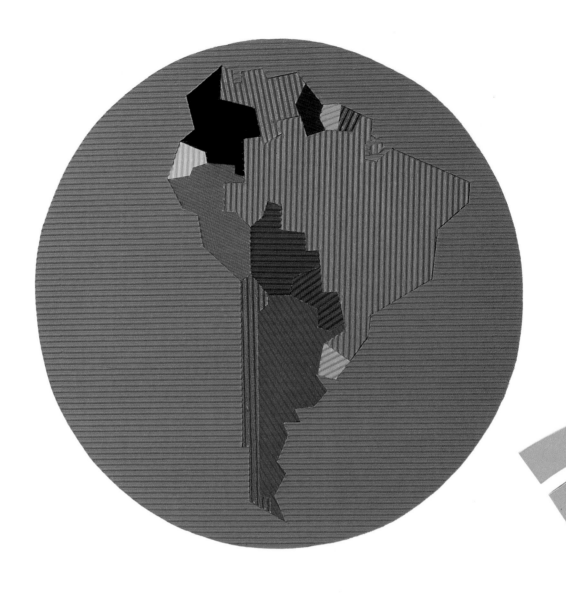

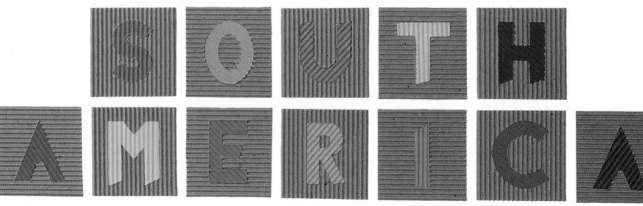

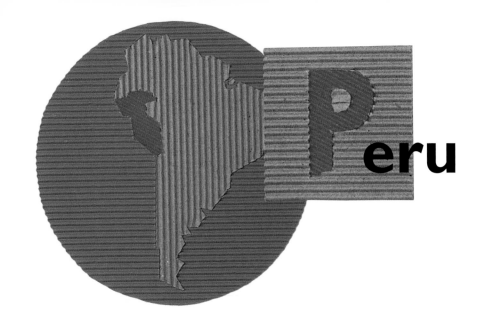

Peru

Condor Airplane

The Condor's Shadow

Long, long ago in the country we now call Peru, the Nazca people worshipped the sun god Viracocha, who they believed had created all life—every bird and fish and tree and human being on earth.

One warm spring day, when the winter had ended and the Nazca were feeling especially grateful to Viracocha, they went to the condor and asked him to carry a message for them. "Tell Viracocha how grateful we are that spring always follows winter," they told the condor. "And thank him for all the beautiful things he has created for us to enjoy on earth."

The condor set off toward the sun with the message. Higher and higher he flew, and his wings spread so wide he cast an enormous shadow on the land. But the closer he got to the sun, the hotter he became. When he could smell his own feathers beginning to singe, and when he saw wisps of smoke rising from his wings, he turned back.

He told the Nazca people, "I couldn't deliver the message. I almost burned up." And he spread one of his wings to show them his singed feathers.

The people had to come up with another way to say thank you to the sun god. Everyone thought and thought, especially the old Nazcas who were supposed to be the wisest of all. One morning a child who loved to draw in the dirt with a stick, making pictures, whispered something into the ear of one of the wise old Nazcas. "It might work," the old Nazca said, and off he went to discuss the child's idea with all the people.

Everyone liked the idea. Well, almost everyone. One old Nazca said that no good idea ever came from a child, but everyone hooted and laughed at her, for they knew children sometimes have the best ideas of all. When they finished laughing, they asked the condor to fly up one more time. As he flew slowly across the sky, they traced the outline of his shadow on the great plain below. From high above, the condor could see a huge drawing of himself on the surface of the earth.

Then the Nazca people drew the outlines of more creatures—a hummingbird, a spider, a lizard, a monkey, and a whale. Soon the whole plain was covered with their drawings, in honor of the sun god. So pleased with the people's beautiful gift was Viracocha, as he looked down from the sky, that he immediately decided to give the Nazca extra-short winters for the next five years.

Tale Tidbits

▶ The South American condor reaches a length of 45 to 55 inches, with a wingspan of 8½ to 10 feet (2.6 to 3 m). Condors weigh between 20 and 25 pounds (9 and 11 kg). They live high in the Andes Mountains and fly as high as 20,000 feet (6,100 m).

▶ The Nazca created the line drawings by removing some of the dark rocks that covered the plain to expose the light desert soil beneath. The giant drawings of the Nazca still exist; if you fly over southern Peru, you can see them on a desert plain overlooking the Nazca Valley.

▶ The story of Viracocha and the condor is one explanation among many of why the Nazca made the drawings. No one yet knows for certain.

How to Make a Condor Airplane

MATERIALS

▶ Cardboard tubes, 1¼, 1¾, and 3¼ inches in diameter
▶ 2-ply cardboard
▶ Clips and rubber bands
▶ Wood glue
▶ Fine, medium, and coarse sandpaper
▶ Wooden dowels, ³⁄₁₆ and ¼ inch in diameter
▶ 5 wooden washers, 1 inch in diameter
▶ Wooden washer, 1¼ inch in diameter
▶ White acrylic gesso
▶ Acrylic paint in desired colors
▶ Tracing paper
▶ Corrugated paper
▶ 2 small tie-rack knobs
▶ Feathers

TOOLS

▶ Pencil
▶ Steel ruler
▶ Cutting knife
▶ Handsaw
▶ Electric drill with ³⁄₁₆, ¼, and ⁵⁄₁₆-inch bits
▶ Paintbrushes

Before you begin: Be sure to read the General Instructions, pages 8–10.

LAUNCHING THE AIRPLANE

PLANE BODY, WINGS, AND TAIL (RED)

1. Cut a 16-inch piece of 3¼-inch tube.
2. Cut a 3¼-inch hole in the top of the tube for the cockpit, 2½ inches from the front edge.
3. Cut a 1¼-inch hole in the bottom of the tube for the back wheel, ⅝ inch from the back edge.
4. Cut a horizontal ¼ x 6-inch slit on each side of the tube, 2 inches from the top and 2½ inches from the front edge, for the wings.
5. Cut a 1¼-inch half circle beneath each slit, ½ inch from the slit's front, for the landing gear.
6. Cut a ¼ x 2½-inch slit in the top for the tail rudder and a horizontal ¼ x 2½-inch slit on each side of the tube, 1¾ inches from the top, for the tail piece.

7. From 6-ply cardboard, cut a wing piece, tail rudder, and tail piece.

COCKPIT (BLUE)

1. Cut two round 3-inch lids from 4-ply cardboard.
2. Cut 1⅛ inch off the side of one lid.

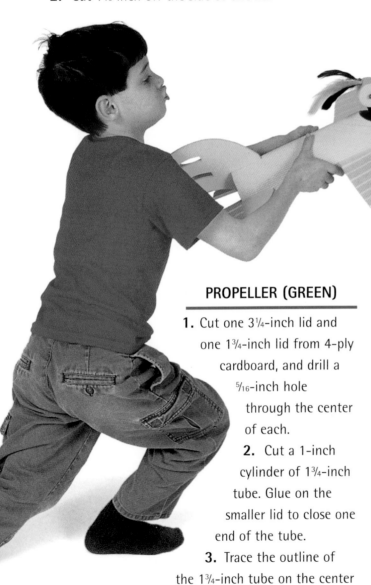

PROPELLER (GREEN)

1. Cut one 3¼-inch lid and one 1¾-inch lid from 4-ply cardboard, and drill a 5⁄16-inch hole through the center of each.
2. Cut a 1-inch cylinder of 1¾-inch tube. Glue on the smaller lid to close one end of the tube.
3. Trace the outline of the 1¾-inch tube on the center of the larger lid.
4. Cut a propeller from 6-ply cardboard, then round and shape the edges with sandpaper. Drill a ¼-inch hole through the center of the propeller.
5. Cut a 3-inch piece of ¼-inch dowel.

FRONT WHEELS AND LANDING GEAR (ORANGE)

1. Cut two 4-inch pieces of 1¼-inch tube. Drill a 5⁄16-inch hole through each piece, ½ inch from the end.
2. Cut two 2½-inch wheels from 6-ply cardboard, then drill a ¼-inch hole through the center of each.
3. Cut a 6-inch piece of ¼-inch dowel.

BACK WHEEL AND LANDING GEAR (PURPLE)

1. Cut a 2½-inch piece of 1¼-inch tube. In one end of the tube, cut a ¾ x 1-inch slit on each side. Shape and round the split end (the wheel cover).
2. Drill a 3⁄16-inch hole through the center of the wheel cover, ¼ inch from the shaped end.
3. Cut a 1¼-inch piece of 3⁄16-inch dowel.

PILOT (LIME)

1. Cut a 1¼-inch piece of 1¾-inch tube for the head. Drill three 1⁄16-inch holes in the top for feathers. Cut a 3⁄16 x ¼-inch slit for the beak.
2. Cut two round 1¾-inch lids from 4-ply cardboard, and drill a 3⁄16-inch hole through the center of each. Glue on the lids to close the head tube.
3. Cut a beak from 4-ply cardboard.
4. Trim the stems off two tie-rack knobs to make eyes.
5. Cut a 2½-inch cylinder of 1¼-inch tube for the neck, and shape one end with sandpaper to fit the curve of the head.

PAINTING AND CORRUGATING

1. Corrugate the body of the plane.
2. Paint the wings and one side of the lids for the cockpit.
3. Corrugate the 3¼-inch propeller lid, except the outlined area.
4. Paint, in this order: the 1¾-inch propeller tube, two 1-inch washers for the propeller gear, two 1-inch washers for the front wheels, tubes for the landing gear, front wheels, a 1¼-inch washer for the rear wheel, then the pilot's head, eyes, beak, and neck.

ASSEMBLING THE CONDOR PLANE

1. Slide the wings, tail rudder, and tail piece into the body slits and glue them in.
2. Glue the half-lid inside the cockpit to close the back of the cockpit. Glue the other lid to the wing, inside the cockpit, to close the front of the cockpit. Paint the inside of the cockpit.
3. Glue the propeller to the ¼-inch dowel, between two 1-inch washers; do not glue the washers yet (see fig. 1). Glue the propeller tube to its outline on the 3¼-inch lid.
4. Slide the dowel through the propeller lids and glue the front 1-inch washer to the dowel, leaving enough space around the propeller for it to rotate easily. Glue the 3¼-inch lid to the front of the plane.
5. Glue the front landing-gear tubes into the plane body and wing. Slide the ¼-inch dowel through

the tubes and glue a front wheel, then a 1-inch washer, on each end of the dowel, leaving some play in the wheels.

6. For the rear wheel, hold the 1¼-inch washer (the wheel) in place inside the wheel cover, and slide the ³⁄₁₆-inch dowel through the wheel cover and the wheel. Glue the dowel in the tube, leaving the wheel free to turn. Glue the rear landing gear into the plane body.
7. Glue, in this order: the beak and eyes in the pilot's head, the feathers in the head, and the head on the body. Glue the pilot in the cockpit.

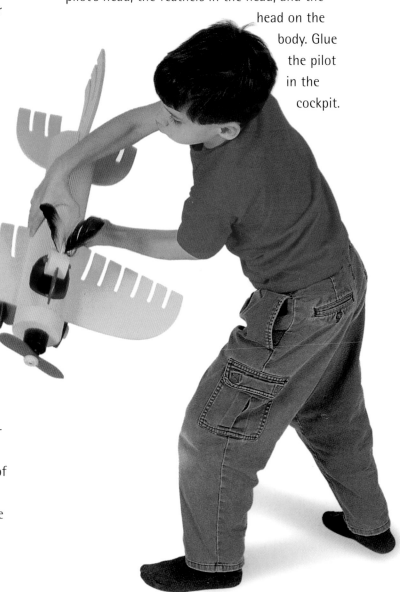

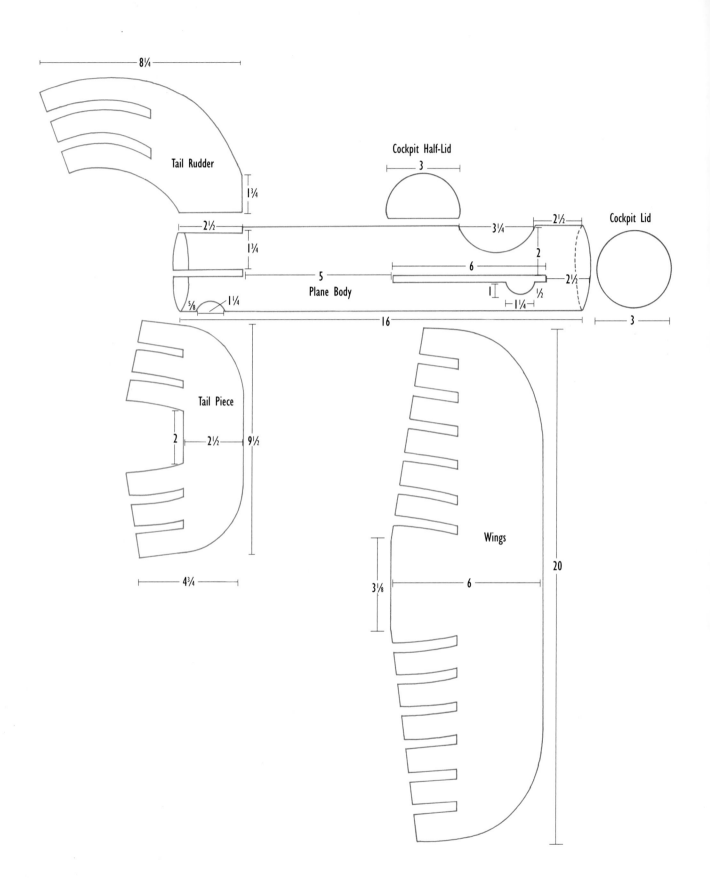

Tail Rudder

8¼

1¾

Cockpit Half-Lid

3

Cockpit Lid

2½

2½

3¼

2

2

6

Plane Body

5

1¾

5⁄8

1¼

I

½

1¼

2½

16

3

Tail Piece

2

2½

9½

4¾

Wings

3⅛

6

20

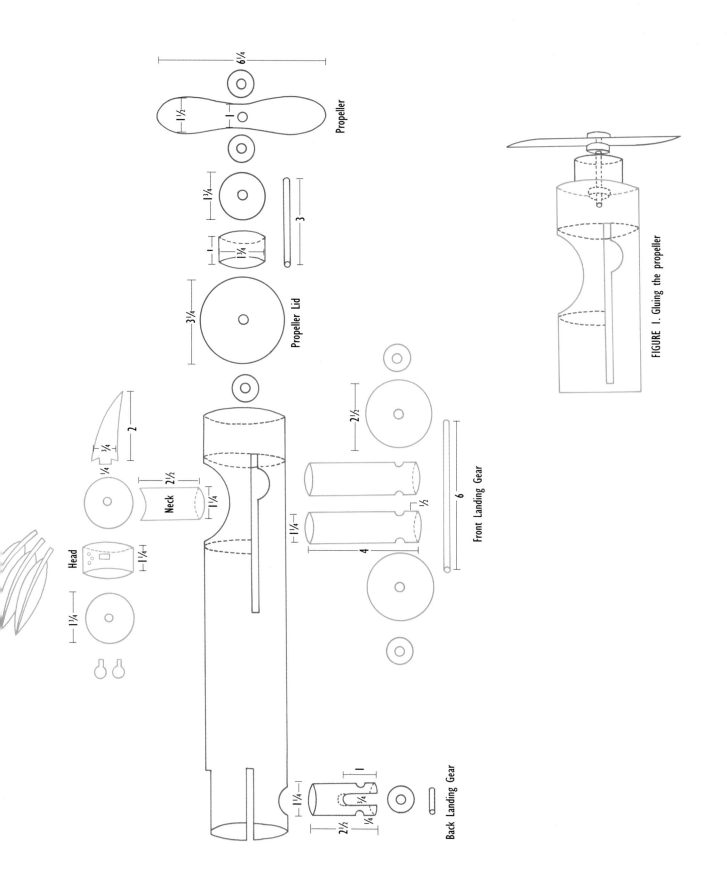

6¼

Propeller

1½

1

1¾

3

1

1¾

3¾

Propeller Lid

2

¾

¼

Neck   2½

1¼

Head

1¼

1¾

2½

1¼

2½

1¼

½

6

4

Front Landing Gear

1¼

1

2½   ¾

¼

Back Landing Gear

FIGURE 1. Gluing the propeller

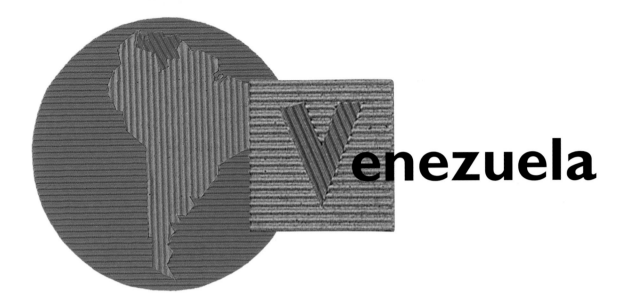

Venezuela

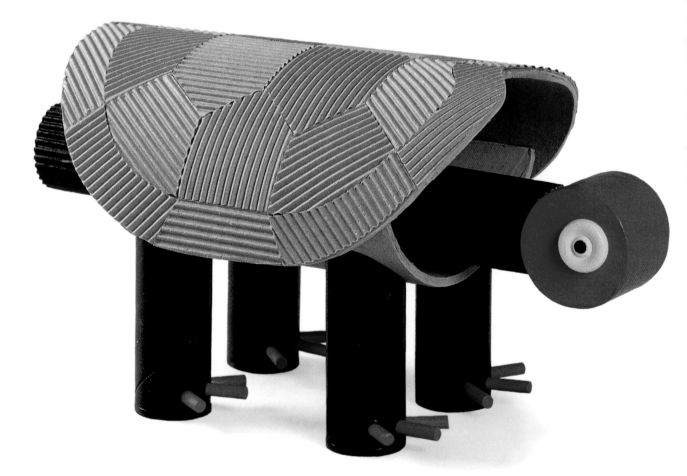

Snake-Neck Turtle

How the Snake-Neck Turtle Got His Shell

A shaman who lived on an island in the sky woke up one day with the feeling he would like to make a special new creature. So after breakfast, he descended to the forest below. He sniffed the fresh forest air. What should he make today? A new kind of fish? A new beautifully colored bird, perhaps one with blue eyes? You don't see many blue-eyed birds, he thought. As he pondered his task, he scooped a handful of mud from the riverbank and found himself molding and shaping it into...a red-headed, snake-neck turtle. He gave the turtle a nice smooth shell and set her in the sun to dry.

Happy with his efforts, the shaman rinsed his hands in the river and went back to his island in the sky to take a vacation after such a hard day's work.

All this time, a very curious spider monkey had hung by his tail from a tall ceiba tree and watched the shaman. After the shaman left, he climbed down, picked up the turtle, and carried her up to a high branch to examine her.

The spider monkey balanced the turtle on the ceiba branch. First he sniffed the turtle. She smelled like warm earth. Then the spider monkey knocked on the turtle's shell. "Turtle! Turtle!" he called. "Come out of there and play with me!"

The turtle poked her head out of her shell. When she saw the spider monkey's face peering at her, she gave a little jerk. For a moment, her shell teetered on the branch like a seesaw. Then it fell down and down and down to the ground.

The spider monkey swung from branch to branch toward the ground, where the turtle lay stunned, her shell broken into many pieces. "The shaman will put a curse on me," the monkey thought, and he raced to a nearby gum tree and collected a handful of sticky gum.

Then, bit by bit, he fit the turtle's shell back together. As careful as he was, the cracks still showed. When the Shaman came down from his island in the sky to check on his newly made turtle, he blinked at the glued-together shell. He blinked again.

High in the ceiba tree, the spider monkey hid and watched, but his trembling made every leaf shake like...a leaf. The monkey swung away into the next tree, and then into the next, and on and on for miles, so he never heard what the shaman said to the snake-neck turtle: "Your new shell is even more beautiful than the one I made for you."

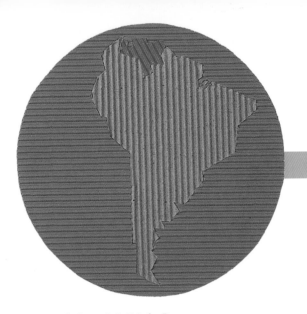

How to Make a Snake-Neck Turtle

MATERIALS

▶ Cardboard tubes, 1¼, 1¾, and 5¼ inches in diameter

▶ 2-ply cardboard

▶ Clips and rubber bands

▶ Wood glue

▶ Wooden dowel, ³/₁₆ inch in diameter

▶ Corrugated paper

▶ Tracing paper

▶ Fine, medium, and coarse sandpaper

▶ 2 wooden washers, ¾ inch in diameter

▶ White acrylic gesso

▶ Acrylic paint in desired colors

▶ 1 foot of string

TOOLS

▶ Pencil

▶ Steel ruler

▶ Cutting knife

▶ Scissors

▶ Handsaw

▶ Electric drill with ³/₁₆-inch bits

▶ Paintbrushes

Before you begin: Be sure to read the General Instructions, pages 8–10.

HATCHING THE TURTLE

SHELL (BLUE)

1. For the top shell, cut out a 5½ x 7½-inch piece of 5¼-inch tube and cut it down the middle (see fig. 1).
2. Shape the piece, rounding the front and rear.
3. For the bottom shell, cut out a 4½ x 5-inch piece of 5¼-inch tube and cut it down the middle, then shape it with sandpaper (see fig. 2).

HEAD AND NECK (RED)

1. Cut a 1½-inch piece of 1¾-inch tube for the head.
2. Cut two round 1¾-inch lids from 4-ply cardboard, and glue them on to close the tube.
3. Cut a 9-inch piece of 1¼-inch tube for the neck, and shape one end to fit the curve of the head. Drill the two ³⁄₁₆-inch holes in the neck tube.
4. Cut a round 1¼-inch lid from 4-ply cardboard, and glue it on to close the back end of the tube.

LEGS (GREEN)

1. Cut four 3-inch pieces of 1¼-inch tube, position them on the outside of the bottom shell, and sand the ends to fit the curve of the shell (see fig. 3).
2. Drill three ³⁄₁₆-inch holes in the front of each leg for toes.
3. From 4-ply cardboard, cut four lids 1¼ inches in diameter.
4. Glue on the lids to close the bottoms of the legs.
5. For toes, cut twelve 1-inch pieces of ³⁄₁₆-inch dowel.

HANGING MECHANISMS (ORANGE)

1. Cut a 1-inch piece of 1¼-inch tube, cut it in half, and drill a ³⁄₁₆-inch hole through the center of each half.
2. Sand the halves to fit the inside curve of the top shell (see fig. 4).

PAINTING AND CORRUGATING

1. To corrugate the top shell, cut brown corrugated paper into a variety of shapes to create a tortoise-shell pattern, then glue them on (see fig. 5).
2. Paint the head. Paint the wooden washers for eyes, and glue one on each side of the head.
3. Corrugate the neck tube and lid.
4. Paint the legs and toes.

ASSEMBLING THE SNAKE-NECK TURTLE

1. Pull a piece of string through each hole in the neck, knot the strings, and pull the knot inside the tube.
2. Pull the strings through the holes of the hanging mechanisms; tie knots, leaving an inch of string between the mechanisms and the neck (see fig. 6).
3. Glue, in this order: the head to the neck, the hanging mechanisms to the inside of the top shell, the bottom shell to the top shell, the toes to the legs, the legs to the bottom shell.

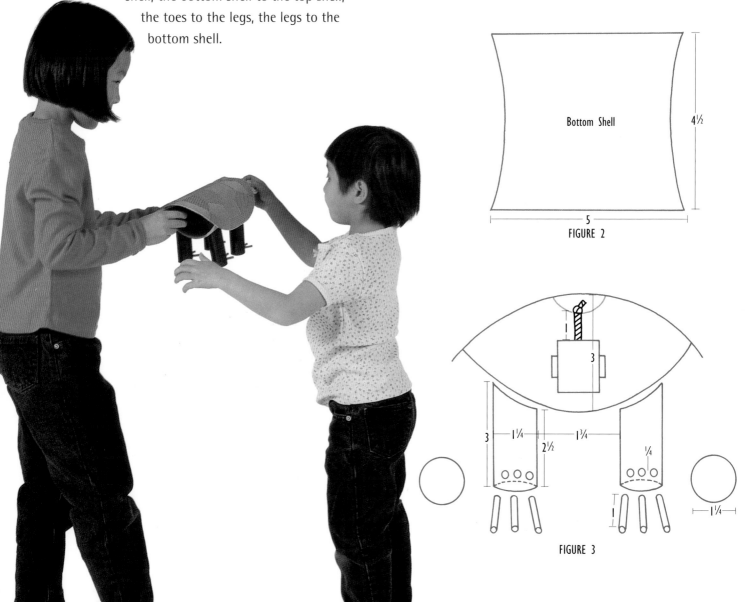

Top Shell

7½

5½

FIGURE 1

Bottom Shell

5

4½

FIGURE 2

3

1¼

2½

1¾

¼

1¼

1

3

1

FIGURE 3

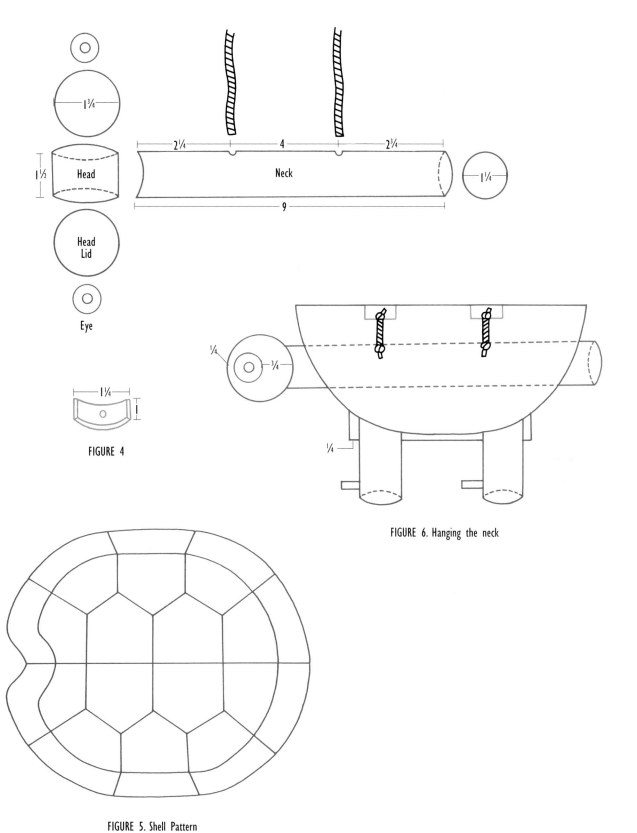

$1\frac{3}{4}$

$1\frac{1}{2}$ | Head

Head
Lid

Eye

$2\frac{1}{4}$ | 4 | $2\frac{3}{4}$

Neck

$1\frac{1}{4}$

9

$1\frac{1}{4}$

1

FIGURE 4

$\frac{1}{4}$ | $\frac{3}{4}$

$\frac{1}{4}$

FIGURE 6. Hanging the neck

FIGURE 5. Shell Pattern

Brazil

Rio Rattles

Carnaval !

In the *favelas* of Rio, it seemed to Reko that everybody was getting ready for Carnaval except him. Even in these poor neighborhoods, where many people lived in shacks made from tin cans or even cardboard, seamstresses sewed bright-colored costumes, dancers worked on their dance steps, and all the bands practiced their fancy marches and happy music.

Reko tried to feel excited. He would be able to watch the parades and enjoy the music. But his mother could not afford to make him a bright costume or buy him rattles to play in a marching band.

Every evening when Reko came inside from watching all the neighbors prepare for Carnaval, he put on a big smile, but his mother saw the sadness in his eyes.

The night before Carnaval, when Reko was fast asleep, his mother pulled from under her bed the materials she had carefully gathered. She filled two empty tin cans with handfuls of black beans and closed them up tight. Then she decorated them with scraps of paper of many bright colors.

She could hardly wait to give her gifts to Reko. Even before the sun came up the next morning, she called softly to her son. "Reko! Reko! Wake up! It's Carnaval, and I have a surprise for you!"

When Reko opened his eyes and crawled out from under his blanket, there sat his mother on her blanket holding out two beautiful rattles. His eyes grew wide. His mouth fell open. He was so surprised he couldn't speak. Instead, he took the rattles from his mother and started shaking them.

Finally his voice returned. "They are beautiful!" he cried out as he danced around the tiny room.

From outside came the sweet piping of whistles and the loud crack of drums. Reko rushed out to join the marching band from his street. Before the band struck up its first joyful tune, all the band members admired Reko's beautiful rattles. Reko couldn't stop smiling. And why should he? It was Carnaval!

Tale Tidbits

▶ The Carnaval of Rio de Janeiro marks the beginning of Lent in February. For a week, all class distinctions disappear and the poor from the favelas, the slums of Rio, become kings and queens.

▶ Marching bands, or Samba Schools, parade through the streets playing the samba, accompanied by dancers in colorful costumes. Each band consists of an array of drums and other percussion instruments.

▶ The Rio Rattles are based on the ganz· or chocalho, shakers or rattles made of tubes filled with beans.

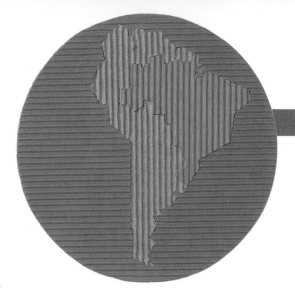

How to Make Rio Rattles

MATERIALS (FOR BOTH RATTLES)

▶ Cardboard tubes, 1, 1¾, and 5¼ inches in diameter; for the Monkey, add a 3¼-inch tube
▶ 2-ply cardboard
▶ Clips and rubber bands
▶ Wood glue
▶ Fine, medium, and coarse sandpaper
▶ Acrylic white gesso
▶ Acrylic paint in desired colors
▶ Corrugated paper
▶ Tracing paper
▶ A handful of small metal bells for the Toucan and dried beans for the Monkey (or your preference)

TOOLS

▶ Pencil
▶ Steel ruler
▶ Cutting knife
▶ Scissors
▶ Hand saw
▶ Paint brushes

Before you begin: Be sure to read the General Instructions, pages 8–10.

HATCHING THE TOUCAN

HEAD AND BEAK (BLUE)

1. Cut a 3-inch piece of 5¼-inch tube, and cut a 1-inch hole centered on the tube. Cut a ⅜ x 1½-inch slit for the beak.
2. Cut two round 5¼-inch lids from 4-ply cardboard, and glue them on to close the head tube.
3. Cut the beak from 8-ply cardboard.

EYES AND EAR COVERTS (LIME)

1. Cut the two ear coverts from 4-ply cardboard.
2. Cut two ½-inch pieces of 1¾-inch tube for eyes. Cut two round 1-inch pupils from 1-ply cardboard. Cut two round 1¾-inch lids from 2-ply cardboard. Glue a pupil on each lid, and glue the lids on to close one end of each eye tube.

HANDLE (RED)

1. Cut a 10½-inch piece of 1-inch tube, sand one end to shape it to the inside curve of the top of the head, and glue it in place.
2. Cut a round 1-inch lid from 4-ply cardboard and glue it to close the bottom of the handle.

PAINTING AND CORRUGATING

1. Paint the sides of the head, except where the ear coverts will be glued. Corrugate the head tube.
2. Paint the edges of the beak, and corrugate the beak except the end that will be inserted into the head.
3. Paint the ear coverts and corrugate them, except the area that will be glued on the face and the area where the eyes will be glued.
4. Paint the eyes, pupils, and handle.

ASSEMBLING THE TOUCAN

1. Glue, in this order: the beak in the head, the ear-coverts to each side of the head, the eyes on the ear coverts.
2. Put a handful of small metal bells in the head.
3. Glue the handle to the inside top of the head.

CAPTURING THE MONKEY

HEAD, MUZZLE, AND EARS (GREEN)

1. Cut a 3-inch piece of 5¼-inch tube for the head, and cut a 1-inch hole centered on the tube.
2. Cut two ¼ x ½-inch slits for ears.
3. Cut two round 5¼-inch lids from 4-ply cardboard, and glue them on to close the head tube.

4. Cut a 2-inch piece of 3¼-inch tube for the muzzle. Cut a round 3¼-inch lid from 4-ply cardboard, and glue it on to close the muzzle tube.
5. Cut the two ears from 6-ply cardboard.

EYES, NOSE, AND MOUTH (ORANGE)

1. Cut two eyebrows from 4-ply cardboard.
2. Cut two ½-inch pieces from 1¾-inch tube for eyes. For the whites of the eyes, cut two round 1¾-inch lids from 2-ply cardboard, and glue them on to close one end of each eye tube. For pupils, cut two round 1-inch lids

   from 2-ply cardboard.
3. Cut a triangle shape from 1¾-inch tube, and sand it to shape the nose.
4. Cut a ½ x 1¾-inch piece of 3¼-inch tube for the mouth.

HANDLE (PURPLE)

1. Cut a 10½-inch piece of 1-inch tube; shape one end to fit the inside curve of the top of the head.
2. Cut a round 1-inch lid from 4-ply cardboard, and glue it on to close the bottom of the handle.

PAINTING AND CORRUGATING

1. Paint the front of the head except where the 3¼-inch muzzle tube and the eyes will be glued. Corrugate the head tube and the back of the head.
2. Paint the front of the muzzle, and corrugate the muzzle tube.
3. Paint the fronts of the ears. Corrugate the edges and backs of the ears.
4. Paint the eyebrows, except where the eyes will be glued, and paint the nose, mouth, and handle.
5. Corrugate the eye tubes.

ASSEMBLING THE MONKEY

1. Glue the pupils on the eyes, glue the eyes to the eyebrows, then glue both eyes to the head.
2. Glue the nose and mouth on the muzzle, and glue the muzzle to the front of the head.
3. Glue the ears in the head.
4. Put a handful of dried beans in the head.
5. Glue the handle to the inside top of the head.

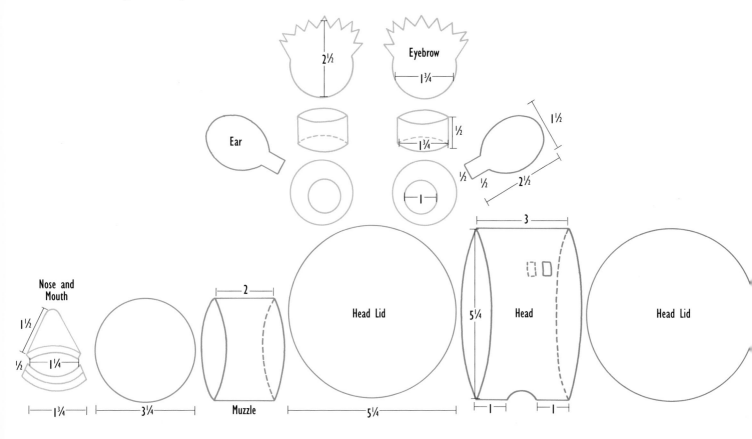

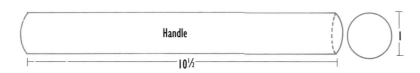

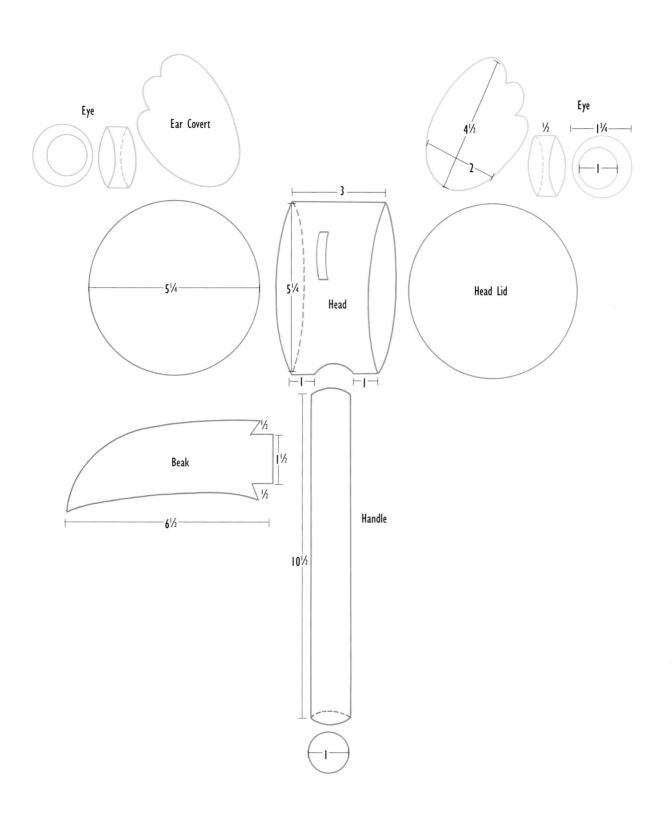

Eye

Ear Covert

Eye

$4\frac{1}{2}$

2

$\frac{1}{2}$

$1\frac{3}{4}$

I

3

$5\frac{1}{4}$

$5\frac{1}{4}$

Head

Head Lid

I

I

Beak

$\frac{1}{2}$

$1\frac{1}{2}$

$\frac{1}{2}$

$6\frac{1}{2}$

Handle

$10\frac{1}{2}$

I

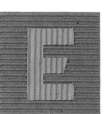

taly

Donato's
Dragon

The Fire-Spitting Dragon

Long, long ago in the town of Euboea lived a very important man in the church, a bishop, whose name was Donato. Nearby, in a cave high on a mountain, lived a dragon. That would have been all right, except every few days the dragon roamed through the town, breathing fire and scaring everyone in the streets.

Each morning and evening and all through the day, Bishop Donato prayed and prayed that the dragon would go away, but instead, one day, the dragon burned down the town. The townspeople yelled at each other that, this time, the dragon had gone too far. Someone had to do something.

But no one knew what to do, so no one did anything.

Donato decided it was up to him. As he started to climb the mountain, panting in the hot sun, a little crowd gathered to cheer him on. But they whispered to each other, "The dragon will turn him into toast."

Below Donato, the ruins of the town smoldered, sending smoke high into the sky. When he finally got to the cave, he shouted, "Come out, you miserable beast!" The mountain rumbled. Donato had woken the dragon. A huge cloud of black smoke poured from the cave and mixed with the smoke from the burning town. The dragon's head poked out of the middle of the smoke. When he saw the bishop, he took a deep breath so that he could spit a long tongue of fire at him and toast him. But Donato was so outraged that a dragon would dare to spit at a bishop, he spat first. Not only did he put out the fire, but the dragon fell over dead.

The townspeople had watched the mountain all day, waiting to see the bishop turned into toast. As the sun set, far up the path they saw a figure climbing slowly toward them. A cheer went up when they recognized Donato. As he drew closer, they saw that he carried in his arms the bones of the fire-breathing dragon. "It's a miracle," they cried to one another. And for his brave and miraculous deed, the church proclaimed Donato a saint.

Tale Tidbits

▶ Many centuries ago, stories traveled around Europe about dragons who roamed the countryside threatening villages and towns. These fearsome beasts were blamed for bringing great disasters upon people, such as earthquakes, wars, famine, and disease.

▶ Donato was the bishop of Euboea, a town in Albania, in the fourth century A.D. For killing a dragon by spitting at it, he was proclaimed Saint Donato. In the 12th century, crusaders took Donato's remains to Venice, where they lie buried in the Basilica of Santa Maria e San Donato, together with the bones of the dragon.

▶ Donato's dragon is modeled on images of dragons from medieval manuscripts.

How to Make Donato's Dragon

MATERIALS

▶ Cardboard tubes, 1½, 1¾, and 3¼ inches in diameter
▶ 2-ply cardboard
▶ Clips and rubber bands
▶ Wood glue
▶ 2 tie-rack knobs
▶ Wooden dowels, ³⁄₁₆ and ¼ inch in diameter
▶ Red foil for flames
▶ String
▶ Fine, medium, and coarse sandpaper
▶ Tracing paper
▶ Corrugated paper
▶ White acrylic gesso
▶ Acrylic paint in desired colors
▶ Wooden washer, ¾ inch in diameter

TOOLS

▶ Pencil
▶ Steel ruler
▶ Cutting knife
▶ Scissors
▶ Handsaw
▶ Electric hand drill with ³⁄₁₆, ¼, and ⁵⁄₁₆-inch bits
▶ Paintbrushes

Before you begin: Be sure to read the General Instructions, pages 8–10.

FIRING UP THE DRAGON

BODY (BLUE)

1. Cut an 8-inch piece of 3-¼-inch tube.
2. Cut a 1¾-inch hole for the neck.
3. Cut a slit ³⁄₁₆ x 3½ inches on top for the plates and a ¼ x 2-inch slit on each side of that slit for wings.
4. Drill a ³⁄₁₆-inch hole behind the plates slit for the tail attachment. Drill two pairs of opposing ¼-inch holes for the leg dowels.
5. Cut a round 3¼-inch lid from 4-ply cardboard, and glue it on to close the front of the body tube.

HEAD, EARS, EYES, AND NECK (GREEN)

1. Cut a 3½-inch piece of 1¾-inch tube for the head. In it, cut two ³⁄₁₆ x ¼-inch slits for ears. Drill two ³⁄₁₆-inch holes for eyes.
2. Cut a round 1¾-inch lid from 4-ply cardboard, and drill a ¼-inch hole through its center. Glue on the lid to close the back of the head tube.

3. Cut the two ears from 4-ply cardboard. Cut the stems from two tie-rack knobs for the eyes, leaving stems no longer than ⅛ inch.
4. Cut a 9-inch piece of 1¾-inch tube for the neck, and sand one end to round and shape it to fit the curve of the head. Cut a ³⁄₁₆ x 4-inch slit for the plates.

FIRE (RED)

1. Cut a 5-inch piece of ³⁄₁₆-inch dowel.
2. Cut strips of foil and glue them to one end of the dowel. Wrap some string around the strips to hold them in place, and glue the string on.
3. Cut a round 1½-inch lid from 4-ply cardboard, then drill a ¼-inch hole through its center.

LEGS AND FEET (ORANGE)

1. Cut four 5-inch pieces of 1½-inch tube for the legs and drill two ¼-inch holes in each tube.
2. Cut four round 1½-inch lids from 4-ply cardboard and glue them on to close the tops of the legs.
3. Cut two 6¼-inch pieces of ¼-inch dowel.
4. Cut four feet from 4-ply cardboard.

TAIL, PLATES, AND WINGS (PURPLE)

1. Cut the tail from 8-ply cardboard and drill a ³⁄₁₆-inch hole vertically through its upper segment.
2. Cut a 3¼-inch piece of ³⁄₁₆-inch dowel.
3. Cut plates for the body and neck from 4-ply cardboard and two wings from 6-ply cardboard.

PAINTING AND CORRUGATING

1. Corrugate the body tube and lid, and corrugate the head tube and lid except where the neck will be glued.
2. Paint the eyes and ears.
3. Corrugate the neck except the area that will be inserted into the body, and corrugate the legs.
4. Paint the feet except the area that will be glued to the legs.
5. Paint the edges of the plates and tail. Corrugate the plates, except the ends that will be inserted into the slits, and corrugate the tail.
6. Paint the edges of the wings. Corrugate the wings except the ends that will be inserted in the body.

ASSEMBLING DONATO'S DRAGON

1. Slide the ¼-inch dowels through the holes in the body and through the legs, and glue them in place (see fig. 1).
2. Glue, in this order: the feet to the legs, the ears in the head, the 1½-inch lid inside the head tube, in front of the ears.
3. Paint the inside of the head.
4. Slide the dowel with the foil flames through the holes in both head lids, and glue a ¾-inch washer to the back of the dowel, outside the head, 1 inch from the end (see fig. 2).
5. Glue, in this order: the eyes in the head, the plates in the neck, the head on the neck, and the neck in the body.
6. Slide the ³⁄₁₆-inch dowel vertically through the hole in the body and tail, and glue it in the hole and to the bottom of the body tube, leaving the tail free to move.
7. Glue the plates and wings in the body.

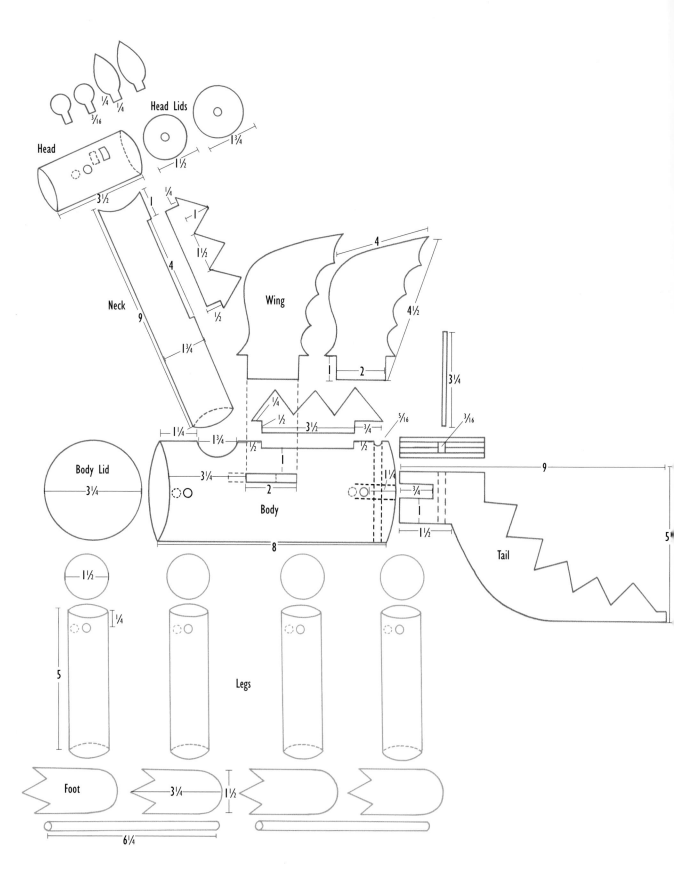

Head Lids

Head

3½

1

¼

1

1½

½

½

Neck

9

4

1¾

Wing

4

4½

1

2

3¼

3/16

3¼

¼

½

3½

¾

5/16

½

Body Lid

3¼

3¼

2

½

1

1¼

Body

¾

1

1½

9

5

Tail

8

1½

¼

Legs

5

Foot

3¼

1½

6¼

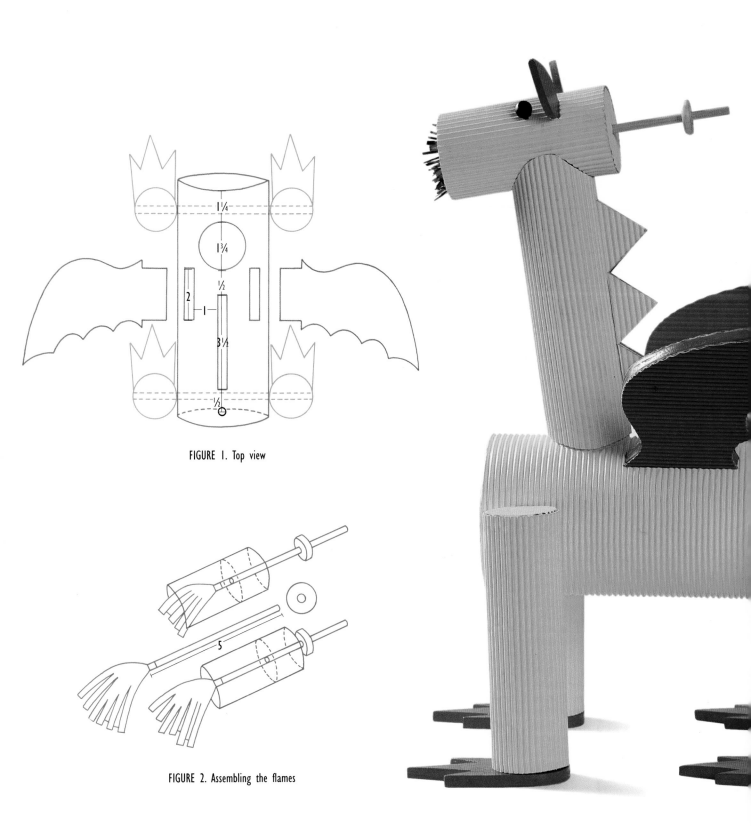

FIGURE 1. Top view

FIGURE 2. Assembling the flames

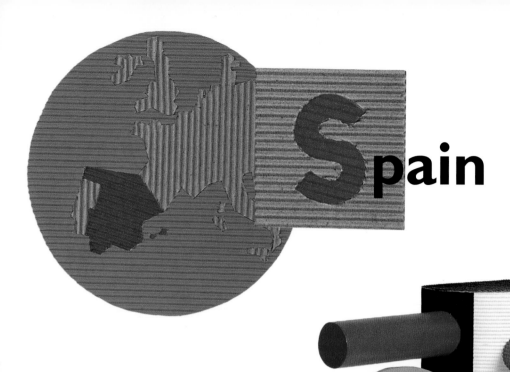

Spain

Pablo
the Bull

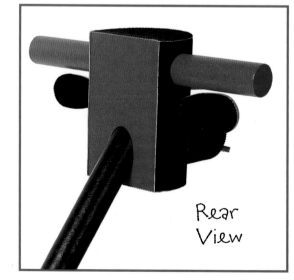

Rear
View

Pablo and the Three Bullies

Pablo was a small, skinny bull with big ears. In bull school all the other bulls bullied him. "You will never fight a matador!" they teased. "Moo! Moo! Moo!" they laughed. One day the headmaster called the bulls together before school. He said," A little town in the province needs a bull for a bullfight. Who wants to go?"

"I'm too big to go to a little town!" said the biggest bull. He flicked his tail, turned up his nose, and pranced away.

"I'm too handsome to go to a little town!" said a bull who looked at himself in the water trough all the time.

"I'm too clever to fight in a little town!" said a bull who always got high marks for his zigzag charges. "We want to fight in the big city!"

"I will go," Pablo said. All the bulls' heads snapped around, and they stared at him out of their sharp brown eyes. Then they all started laughing and hooting. "Ha, ha, ha! Moo! Moo! Moo!" Pablo had never felt so lonely and ashamed.

On the day of the bullfight, everyone in the little town came. All the stores closed. Everyone stopped working. The schoolmaster even called off school. The townspeople crowded into the stands of the little bullring. A band played, with lots of tooting of horns and loud drums. First the matador came into the ring. Everyone in the stands stood up and cheered. When Pablo entered the ring, the crowd cheered even louder, and two people fainted from excitement.

Tale Tidbits

▶ The first bullfights were held in public squares. As the art of bull-fighting gained in popularity, special bullrings were built and special bulls were bred for the fights.

▶ Bullfighting has spread from Spain to France and Portugal, and through-out Latin America.

▶ Pablo the Bull is based on the wooden bulls on wheels that young bullfighters or matadors use to prac-tice the art of bullfighting.

Pablo danced around the matador's cape and brushed the matador with his horns. "Olé!" the crowd cheered. Pablo swung around and charged again at the red cape. He lifted the matador up with his horns and threw him into the stands! The matador landed right in the laps of the musicians.

"Bravo! Bravo, Pablo!" the crowd shouted and applauded. Pablo bent his front legs and bowed. Señoritas threw beautiful red and yellow roses into the ring. As the soft shower of roses fell on Pablo, he felt happy.

By the time Pablo returned to bull school, all the bulls had heard about his triumph in the ring. They were still too proud to apologize to him. But the clever bull asked him how he had caught the matador on his horns. And none of the bulls ever bullied Pablo again.

How to Make Pablo the Bull

MATERIALS

▶ Cardboard tubes, 1¼, 1½, 3¼, and 5¼ inches in diameter
▶ 2-ply cardboard
▶ Clips and rubber bands
▶ Fine, medium, and coarse sandpaper
▶ Wood glue
▶ Wooden dowel, ⁵⁄₁₆ inch in diameter
▶ White acrylic gesso
▶ Acrylic paint in desired colors
▶ Corrugated paper
▶ Tracing paper

TOOLS

▶ Pencil
▶ Steel Ruler
▶ Cutting knife
▶ Scissors
▶ Handsaw
▶ Electric hand drill with ⅜-inch and ⁵⁄₁₆-inch bits
▶ Paintbrushes

Before you begin: Be sure to read the General Instructions, pages 8–10.

RELEASING THE BULL

HEAD (BLUE)

1. Cut a 7-inch piece of 5¼-inch tube, and draw a vertical line down its length. Starting at the line, measure 10 inches around the tube and draw another vertical line the length of the tube. Cut along both lines to open the back of the head tube.

2. For the horns/handles, cut a hole 1½ inches in diameter on the upper part of each side of the head. Below each hole, cut a vertical slit ³⁄₁₆ x ½ inch for the ears.

3. Cut two round 5¼-inch lids from 4-ply cardboard. Cut a piece 1¾ inches off each lid. Glue the remaining partial lids, now 3½ inches across, on the top and bottom of the head to close the ends off.

4. Cut a 5 x 7-inch piece of 4-ply cardboard, for the back of the head. Cut an oval hole 1½ inches wide in it, centered and ⅜ inch from the bottom, for the pole (see fig. 1). Glue the piece on the back of the head.

NOSE, MOUTH, AND TONGUE (RED)

1. Cut a 3-inch piece of 3¼-inch tube for the nose. Sand one end to fit the curve of the head.

2. Cut a round 3¼-inch lid from 4-ply cardboard. Drill two ⅜-inch nose holes in the lid, and cut a ³⁄₁₆ x 1-inch slit for the tongue. Glue the lid on the nose tube.

3. Draw an outline of the 3¼-inch nose tube on the face.

4. Cut the tongue from 4-ply cardboard.

EYES, EARS, AND HORNS (GREEN)

1. Cut two 1-inch pieces of 1¼-inch tube for the eyes. Sand one end of each cylinder to fit the curve of the face. Draw an outline of the eyes on the face.

2. Cut two ears from 4-ply cardboard.

3. Cut a 15½-inch piece of 1½-inch tube for the horns/handles. Cut two round 1½-inch lids from 4-ply cardboard, and glue on the lids to close the ends of the horns/handles.

POLE AND WHEEL (ORANGE)

1. Cut a 36-inch piece of 1½-inch tube for the pole. Drill two opposite ⁵⁄₁₆-inch holes through the tube, ½ inch from the end.

2. Cut two ½ x 2½-inch slits for the wheel mount.

3. Cut a round 1½-inch lid from 4-ply cardboard. Cut a ½-inch part-circle off each side. Glue the part-circles on each side of the slit.

4. Cut a 3¼-inch wheel from 8-ply cardboard. Drill a ⅜-inch hole through the center.

5. Cut a 1½-inch piece of ⁵⁄₁₆-inch dowel.

PAINTING AND CORRUGATING

1. Paint the back of the head. Corrugate the top and bottom of the head except for the outlined areas.

2. Corrugate the 3¼-inch nose tube and lid.

3. Paint the edges and fronts of the ears. Corrugate the backs of the ears, except the ends that will be inserted in the head.

4. Paint the edge of the tongue; corrugate the top and bottom.

5. Paint the edges of the eyes; corrugate the eye tubes.

6. Paint the horns, pole, and wheel.

ASSEMBLING PABLO THE BULL

1. Slide the horns through the holes in the head.

2. Glue, in this order: ears in the head, nose tube on the face, tongue in the slit, and eyes on the face.

3. Slide the wheel into the pole slit, then slide the dowel through the pole and wheel.

4. Glue the dowel in the pole, leaving the wheel free to turn.

5. Slide the pole through the hole in the back of the head, and glue it.

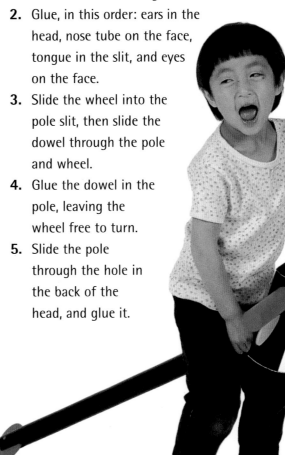

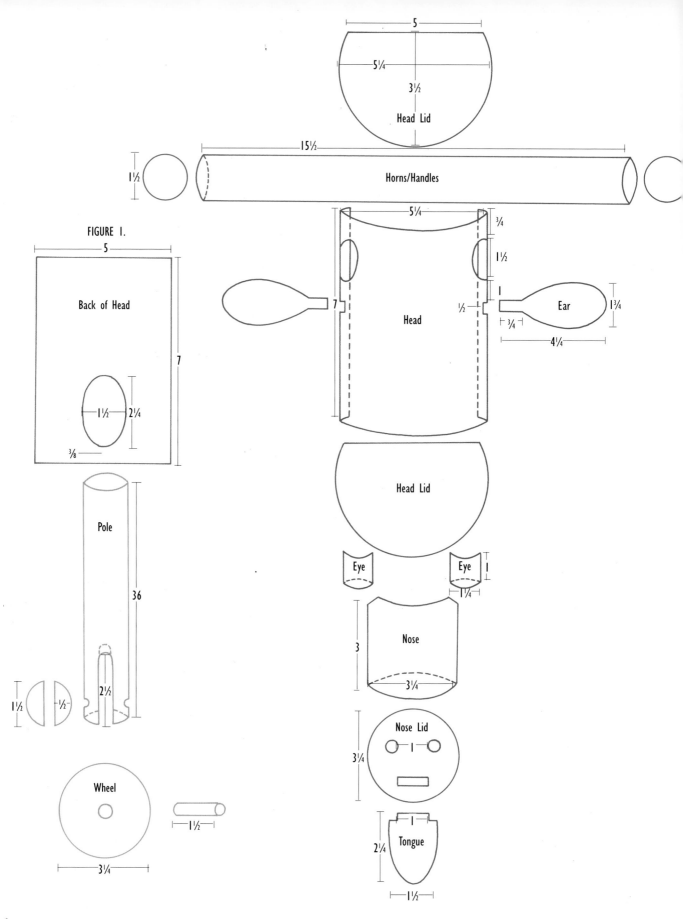

5

5¼

3½

Head Lid

15½

1½

Horns/Handles

FIGURE I.

5

Back of Head

7

5¼

¾

1½

1

½

Head

7

Ear

1¾

¾

4¼

1½

2¼

⅜

Head Lid

Pole

Eye

Eye

1

36

1¼

Nose

3

2½

1½

½

3¼

Nose Lid

3¼

Wheel

1½

Tongue

2¼

3¼

1

1½

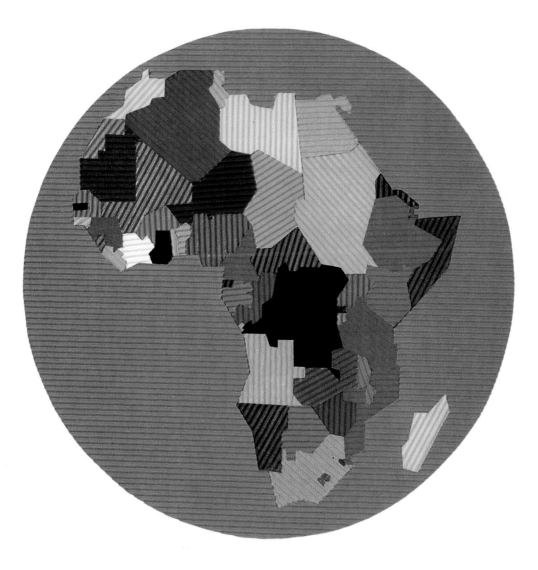

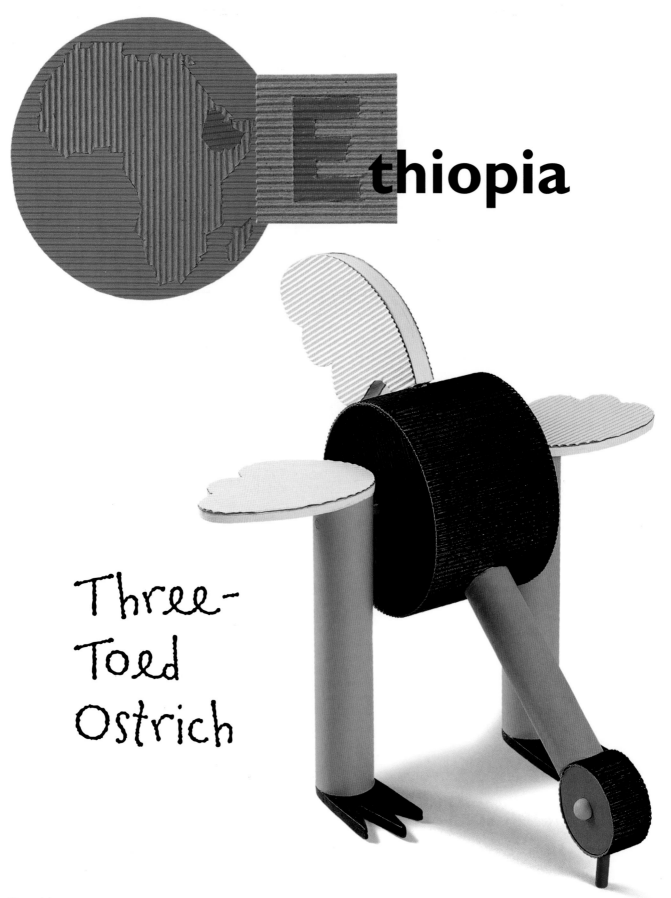

Ethiopia

Three-Toed Ostrich

The Scrawny Ostrich

From the throne room of the great palace in Aksum, the word went out: The king needed the finest ostrich feathers in the land to decorate his new crown. The most observant of the king's trusted servants went to the city's market in search of the most beautiful, softest, longest white plumes from the tail of a stately male ostrich.

In a dark corner of the market, they came upon the only ostrich to be found. The small, dusty three-toed ostrich trembled in a corner of its cage. "What a scruffy, ugly bird!" one of the servants said. The crowd that had followed the king's servants through the market hooted and laughed.

"What a scrawny fellow!" said another servant, showing off for the crowd.

"With three toes!" mocked a third servant, doubling over with laughter himself. "Everyone knows ostriches have only two toes!"

At that moment an old man stepped out of the crowd and bought the little ostrich. The servants and the crowd made fun of him as he loaded the cage onto his handmade cart and wheeled the ostrich away. "They're perfect for each other! Both of them skinny and scrawny!"

The old man wheeled the little ostrich far beyond the city walls and set him free on the plains. There the three-toed ostrich ate plants, with plenty of sand and gravel to help him digest them. He grew to nearly eight feet tall, which is as tall as ostriches ever get.

Thick, sleek black feathers covered his back, and plumes fluffy as cotton waved from his tail.

Years passed, and word of a beautiful ostrich that lived far beyond the city walls reached the palace in Aksum. The king ordered that the ostrich be captured, so that its handsome feathers could be plucked to decorate his crown and make grand fans for his lowest servants to cool him with. When the ostrich was brought before the king, the observant servants were too embarrassed to look at each other. Inside, each one was saying to himself, "How stupid those other servants were! It is that three-toed ostrich the old man bought years ago!"

The king gazed at the ostrich, who stood tall and proud as a king himself. "I hate to admit it," the king said, "but his feathers look even more handsome on him than they would in my crown." And he ordered the bird returned to his home on the plains, where he sired generations of handsome ostriches, every one with an extra toe.

Tale Tidbits

▶ Ostriches live throughout east Africa on the plains and deserts.

▶ Aksum was the ancient capital of the kingdom of Ethiopia and an important trading center for incense, spices, gold, ivory, and ostrich feathers.

▶ The Ethiopians used ostrich feathers to make fans and to decorate the crowns of kings and queens.

▶ Although ostriches cannot fly, their long legs take steps 15 feet (4.5 meters) long, and they can run at speeds up to 40 miles (65 kilometers) an hour. The insulting notion that ostriches bury their heads in sand is untrue.

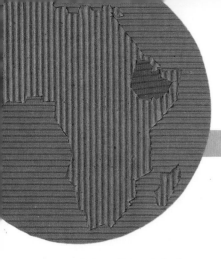

How to Make a Three-Toed Ostrich

MATERIALS

- Cardboard tubes, 1¼, 1½, 2¼, and 5¼ inches in diameter
- 2-ply cardboard
- Clips and rubber bands
- Fine, medium, and coarse sandpaper
- Wood glue
- Wooden dowels, ¼ and ⁵⁄₁₆ inch in diameter
- 2 wooden balls, ½ inch in diameter
- Tracing paper
- Corrugated paper
- White acrylic gesso
- Acrylic paint in desired colors
- 2½ cups uncooked rice

TOOLS

- Pencil
- Steel ruler
- Cutting knife
- Scissors
- Handsaw
- Electric hand drill with ¼ and ⁵⁄₁₆-inch bits
- Paintbrushes

Before you begin: Be sure to read the General Instructions, pages 8–10.

HATCHING THE OSTRICH

BODY (BLUE)

1. Cut a 3½-inch piece of 5¼-inch tube. Cut a 1-¼-inch hole for the neck and a ½ x ⅝-inch slit for the tail.

2. Make two round 5¼-inch lids, and drill a ⁵⁄₁₆-inch hole through the center of each. Glue one lid on each side to close the tube.

TAIL, LEGS, FEET, AND WINGS (RED)

1. Cut the tail from 10-ply cardboard.
2. For the legs, cut two 8-inch pieces of 1½-inch tube, and drill a ¼-inch hole all the way through ½ inch from the end of each piece.
3. Cut a 7½-inch piece of ¼-inch dowel.
4. Cut the two feet and two wings from 6-ply cardboard.

HEAD AND NECK (LIME)

1. Cut a 1-inch piece of 2¼-inch tube, then drill a ⁵⁄₁₆-inch hole centered on it for the beak.
2. Make two round 2¼-inch lids from 4-ply cardboard, and drill a ³⁄₈-inch hole through the center of each. Glue one lid on each side to close the tube.
3. Cut a 3-inch piece of ⁵⁄₁₆-inch dowel for the beak.
4. Cut an 8-inch piece of 1¼-inch tube for the neck, and sand one end of it to fit the curve of the head.
5. Cut a round 1¼-inch lid from 2-ply cardboard, then glue it on to close one end of the neck.

PAINTING AND CORRUGATING

1. Corrugate the body.
2. Paint the edge of the tail, then corrugate the tail on both sides, except the end that will be inserted into the body.
3. Paint the sides of the head, then corrugate the head tube, except the area where the neck will be glued.
4. Paint, in this order: the neck, legs, and feet (except the area where the legs will be glued).
5. Paint the edge and underside of the wings; corrugate the tops.
6. Paint the two wooden balls for eyes and the dowel for the beak.

ASSEMBLING THE THREE-TOED OSTRICH

1. Slide the 7½-inch piece of dowel through the body and legs, then glue it to the legs, leaving space between the legs and body so that the body can bob freely.
2. Glue the feet to the bottoms of the legs and the wings to the tops of the legs.
3. Glue the tail in the slit in the body.
4. Put 1½ cups of rice into the body.
5. Glue the beak in the head. For extra weight, fill the head with rice through the holes.
6. Glue the eyes in the head. For extra weight, fill the neck with rice, then glue the head on the neck.
7. Slide the neck through the hole in the body, and adjust its length to counterbalance the weight of the tail, so that the ostrich can stand head up. Glue the neck at this position.

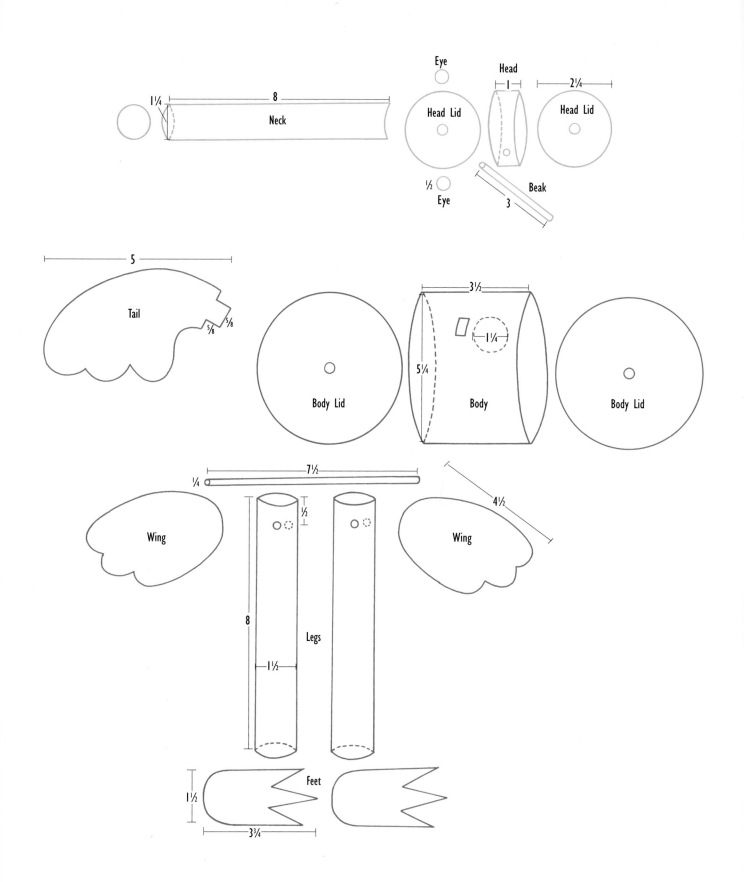

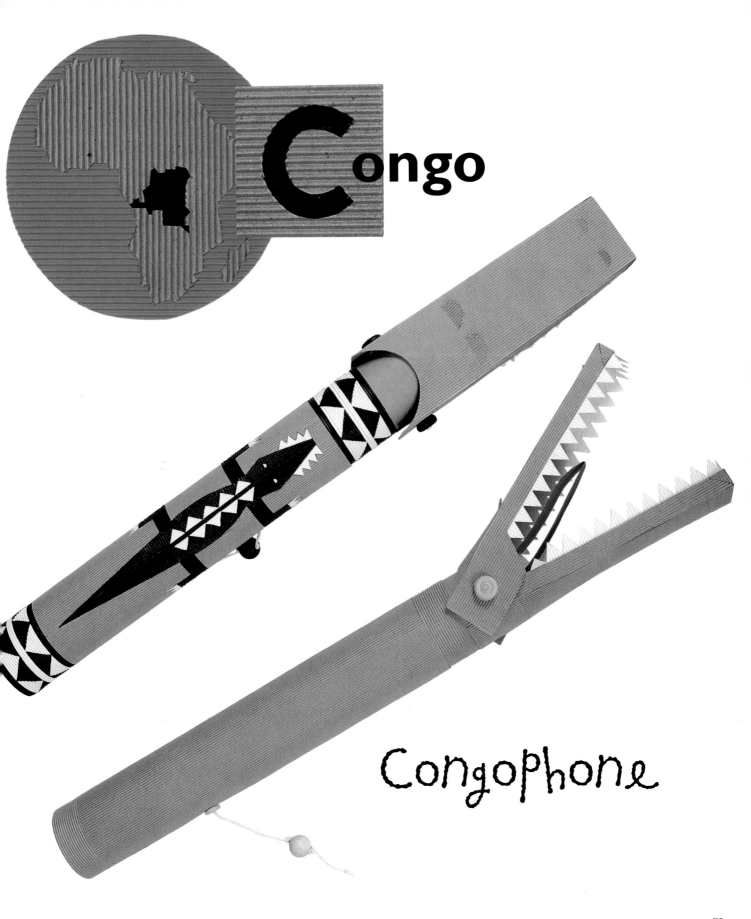

Congo

Congophone

Better than a Cordless Phone

Moke and Okeke walked from their village to the big city to sell fruit at the market. When every piece of fruit was gone, they wandered through the city to look in the windows of all the exciting shops—bakeries and toy shops, music stores and hardware shops, pet stores and stores that sold nothing but hats or shoes.

At an electronics store they pressed their faces against the window. Moke pointed to a cordless phone. "I want one of those," he said. "I could call you from anyone's house, or from the river to tell you to come swimming."

"Yes, I want one too!" Okeke said.

Moke and Okeke counted their money, but they did not have enough to buy even one cordless phone.

That evening when they returned home, they told their uncle Nokeke about the cordless phone.

"Oh, that is nothing," their uncle Nokeke said. "I have something much better!" And he reached under the bed and pulled out two long wooden tubes shaped like crocodiles.

Moke jumped back. "What are those?" he cried out. He felt a little embarrassed about being scared. "You surprised me, pulling those out so fast," he told his uncle. Okeke giggled.

"These are Congophones," said Uncle Nokeke. "With these you can also talk to people who are far away. And you can call each other to go swimming whenever you want to. But even more than that—" Uncle Nokeke looked around as if he didn't want anyone else to hear.

"What? What?" Okeke and Moke pulled on his shirt.

"You don't need batteries," said Uncle Nokeke. "And, even better than that—" He got up and closed the door.

"Tell us! Tell us!" cried Okeke and Moke.

"With Congophones," whispered Uncle Nokeke, "you can talk to the animals in the forest!"

The next day Moke and Okeke talked to the crocodiles on the Congophones. They talked to the monkeys high in the trees. Then they went for a swim.

Tale Tidbits

▶ Hunters in the Congo used a megaphone to communicate messages to each other.

▶ The Congophones are based on a traditional megaphone used throughout the Congo River basin. One such megaphone, collected at the end of the 19th century, is on display at the Pigorini Museum in Rome. It is made of wood and carved in the shape of a crocodile.

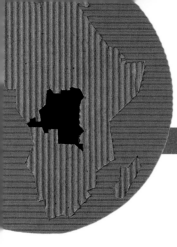

How to Make a Congophone

MATERIALS

- A piece of oak ¾ x ¾ x 3⅛ inches (or any wood of about the same weight)
- Fine, medium, and coarse sandpaper
- Cardboard tube, 3¼ inches in diameter
- Wooden dowel, ¼ inch in diameter
- 5 wooden washers, ¾ inch in diameter
- Wood glue
- Tracing paper
- Corrugated paper
- White string, 3 feet long
- Wooden ball, ¾ inch in diameter
- White corrugated paper
- White acrylic gesso (optional)
- Acrylic paint in desired colors (optional)
- 2 wooden washers, 1 inch in diameter

TOOLS

- Pencil
- Steel ruler
- Cutting knife
- Scissors
- Handsaw
- Electric hand drill with ¹³⁄₆₄, ³⁄₁₆, ¼, and ⁵⁄₁₆-inch bits
- Paintbrushes (optional)

Before you begin: Be sure to read the General Instructions, pages 8–10.

CONNECTING THE CONGOPHONE

TUBE AND MOVING MECHANISM (BLUE)

1. Drill a ¼-inch hole and a 1³/₆₄-inch hole through the piece of wood (see fig. 1).

2. Cut a 23-inch piece of 3¼-inch tube, and drill two opposite ⁵/₁₆-inch holes through the tube 1¼ inches from the front edge.

3. Cut a 4¾-inch piece of ¼-inch dowel.

4. Drill a ¼-inch hole in the center of each of the five washers.

5. Place the wood inside the tube and slide the dowel through the tube, through one ¾-inch washer, through the wood, through another ¾-inch washer, and out the other side of the tube (see fig. 2). Glue the wood in the middle of the dowel between the washers.

6. Glue a ¾-inch washer to each end of the dowel on the outside of the tube, leaving space between the washers and the tube (see fig. 2).

7. Corrugate the tube except the 2¾ inches from the front edge.

8. Drill a ³/₁₆-inch hole in the bottom of the tube, 6½ inches from the end. Glue a ¾-inch washer on the hole.

9. Thread string through the hole in the rear of the tube, leaving 10 inches outside the tube (see fig. 3). Thread the other end through the ¹³/₆₄-inch hole in the wood, and knot it to hold it in place.

10. Drill a ³/₁₆-inch hole through the wooden ball. Tie a knot in the string hanging outside the rear of the tube, thread the ball onto the string, and tie another knot to hold it in place (see fig. 3).

HEAD AND EYES (RED)

1. Draw the top jaw/head on corrugated paper and cut it out.

2. Cut around the solid lines for the eyelids and nose holes. On the corrugated side of the paper, score lightly along the dotted lines for the eyelids and nose holes and fold the semicircles up.

3. On the smooth side of the paper, score lightly along the remaining dotted lines and fold the sides and end up. Glue the front flaps around the sides of the upper jaw.

4. Draw the lower jaw on corrugated paper and cut it out. On the corrugated side of the paper, score lightly along the dotted lines and fold the sides and ends down. Glue the front flaps around the sides of the lower jaw.

5. Draw the eyes on white corrugated paper and cut them out.

TEETH AND TONGUE (GREEN)

1. Draw the teeth and gums on white corrugated paper, 28 teeth for the top jaw, 27 teeth for the bottom jaw. Cut out the teeth/gum pieces.
2. Draw the tongue on corrugated paper, cut it out, fold it, and paint it.

ASSEMBLING THE CONGOPHONE

1. Glue the 28 teeth in the top jaw, with 4 teeth in front. Glue the 27 teeth in the lower jaw, with 3 teeth in front (fig. 4).
2. Glue, in this order: the eyes (corrugated side up) inside the upper jaw, the lower jaw to the tube, the tongue to the piece of wood (see fig. 5).
3. Attach the upper jaw/head to the dowel and glue it to the washers.
4. With the tongue lying on the bottom of the mouth and the mouth closed, glue a 1-inch washer (red) on each end of the dowel, leaving space for the upper jaw to move freely (see figs. 6 and 7).

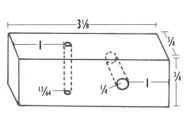

FIGURE 1. Drilling the wood

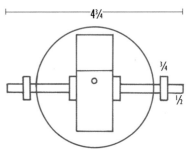

FIGURE 2. Gluing the wood

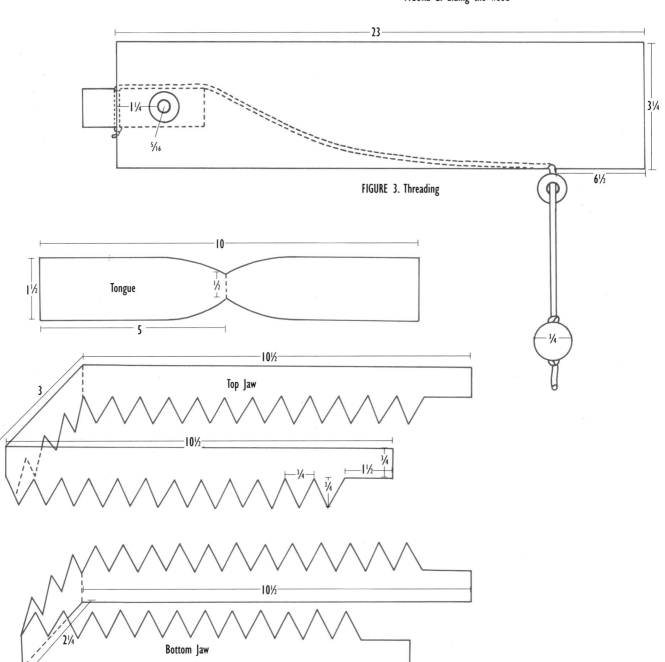

FIGURE 3. Threading

Tongue

Top Jaw

Bottom Jaw

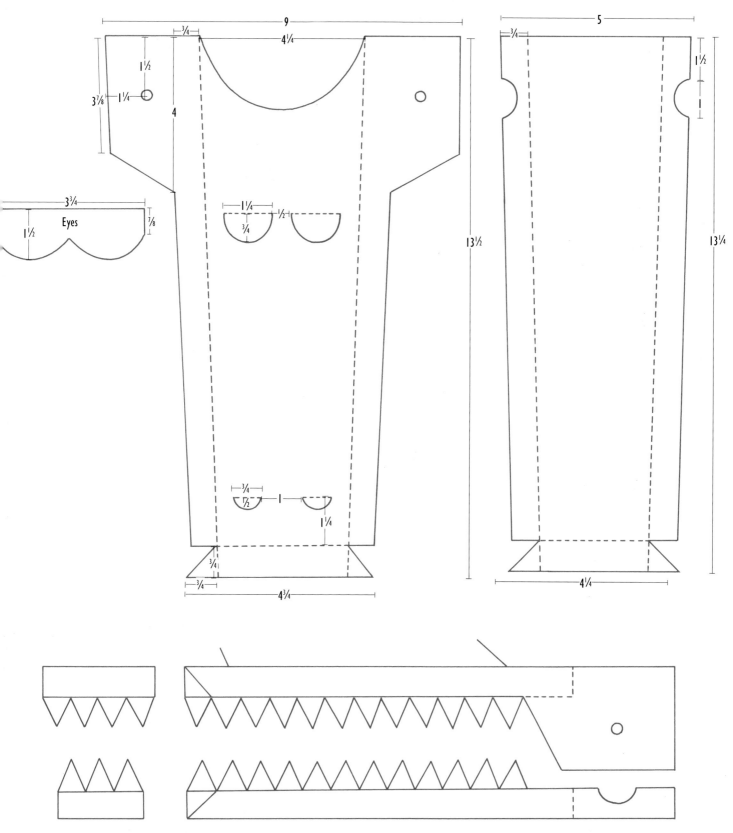

FIGURE 4. Gluing the Teeth

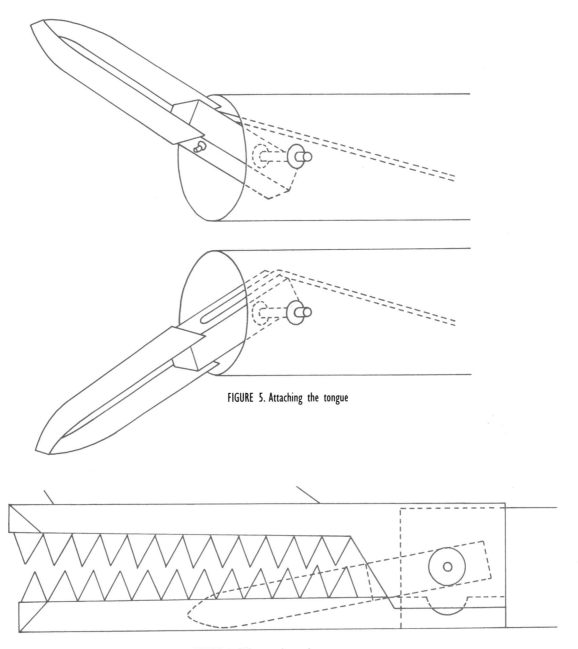

FIGURE 5. Attaching the tongue

FIGURE 6. Gluing on the washers

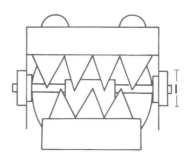

FIGURE 7. Front view

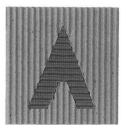

China

Yan Shih's Puppet Theater

The Puppet Who Winked

Yan Shih was a master puppeteer who made such fine puppets, he was invited to perform puppet plays at the court of the emperor Mu Wang. For one play, Yan Shih made puppets that looked exactly like the emperor and his daughter. The emperor was delighted! He called the whole court together to watch Yan Shih's new play.

When everyone had settled quietly in front of the puppet theater, Yan Shih told a story with his puppets. In the story, a young knight came to the palace to seek the hand of the emperor's daughter in marriage.

The emperor was fascinated by the story, and he never took his eyes off the puppets. Yan Shih was so skilled at his art that the emperor became convinced that the puppets were real. As he watched the knight woo his daughter, for a moment the emperor thought he saw the young man wink at the princess.

The emperor was furious. Who did this young knight think he was? No one ever winks at an emperor's daughter! What a lack of respect! His face bright red with anger, the emperor called for his chief executioner. But did he order the executioner to kill the knight? No, he ordered his chief executioner to kill Yan Shih for bringing such a rude knight into his court.

Before the executioner could grab him, Yan Shih turned the knight puppet sideways so the emperor could see that he was merely a puppet, made only of wood and paper.

The emperor remembered he was watching a play. He cleared his throat and stared around at the members of his court, daring anyone to laugh at his mistake. No one did. But as the king waved his hand at Yan Shih, telling him to go on with the play, some of the young people in the court nudged each other with their elbows, where the emperor couldn't see them. Yan Shih might be a master puppeteer, but imagine an emperor mistaking a puppet play for real life!

Tale Tidbits

▶ The Chinese puppet theater has evolved over the centuries into a highly developed art form.

▶ Rod puppets like those in Yan Shih's Theater are the most popular in China of the many kinds of puppets that exist. Chinese puppets are elaborately painted and dressed to appear lifelike.

▶ There is a saying in China: "There are 360 professions in the world, but the hardest to master is that of the puppeteer." In other words, becoming a puppet master takes a lot of practice.

▶ Yan Shih's Puppet Theater is based on the traditional Chinese puppet theater. The puppets include the emperor, in red with a black beard; the emperor's daughter, with a fan; the knight, on horseback; and the chief executioner, with a mask and a white beard.

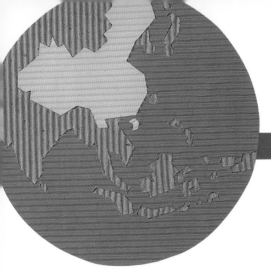

How to Make Yan Shih's Puppet Theater

MATERIALS (FOR 4 PUPPETS)

- 4 wooden eggs
- 2 wooden dowels, ¼ inch in diameter
- Wood glue
- White acrylic gesso
- Acrylic paint in desired colors
- For decorations: felt scraps, tassels, pipe cleaners, and small pom-poms
- Red, black, yellow, and white felt
- Corrugated paper
- 2-ply cardboard
- Clips and rubber bands
- Tracing paper
- Fine, medium, and coarse sandpaper
- Cardboard tube, 3¼ x 33 inches

TOOLS

- Pencil
- Steel ruler
- Cutting knife
- Scissors
- Handsaw
- Electric hand drill with a ¼-inch bit
- Paintbrushes

Before you begin: Be sure to read the General Instructions, pages 8–10.

OPENING NIGHT

Note: All four puppets are made in the same way. They differ only in the ways they are decorated.

PUPPET HEAD (BLUE)

1. In a wooden egg, drill a ¼-inch hole, ½ inch deep, for the neck.

2. Cut a 14-inch piece of ¼-inch dowel, then glue it in the hole in the egg (see fig.1).

3. Paint a face and hair on the egg. For male characters, cut beards from felt and glue them on (see fig. 1).

HEADDRESS (PURPLE)

1. Cut two strips of corrugated paper, 5¼ x 1¼ inches and ½ x 1¼ inches. Make the longer strip into a cylinder, then glue its ends to the small piece (see fig. 2a).

2. Draw a headdress on corrugated paper and cut it out, then paint and decorate it with small pom-poms, pipe cleaners, and tassels (see fig. 2b).

3. Glue the headdress to the smaller strip of corrugated paper (see fig. 2c).

COSTUME (RED)

1. Cut a costume from 4-ply cardboard. (The knight's costume includes the horse.) For the emperor's daughter, cut out a fan from 2-ply cardboard.

2. Paint the back of the costume or cover it with Chinese-motif paper, and corrugate the front.

3. For the knight's lance (lime), cut a 7-inch piece of ¼-inch dowel, paint it, glue a pom-pom on one end, and glue the dowel to the back of the horse.

4. Cut tabs of corrugated paper (orange) to attach the costume to the dowel (see fig. 3).

5. Glue the dowel to the back of the costume, then glue the tabs over the dowel and the costume.

6. Glue the headdress on the head.

PUPPET THEATER (GREEN AND PINK)

1. Cut two 16½-inch pieces of 3¼-inch tube for the pillars (green)

2. Make a ¼ x 1½ inch slit in each pillar, opposite each other.

3. Cut a roof from 6-ply cardboard (pink).

4. Paint the pillars and corrugate the front of the roof except the area that will be inserted in the slits.

5. Slide the roof into the pillar slits.

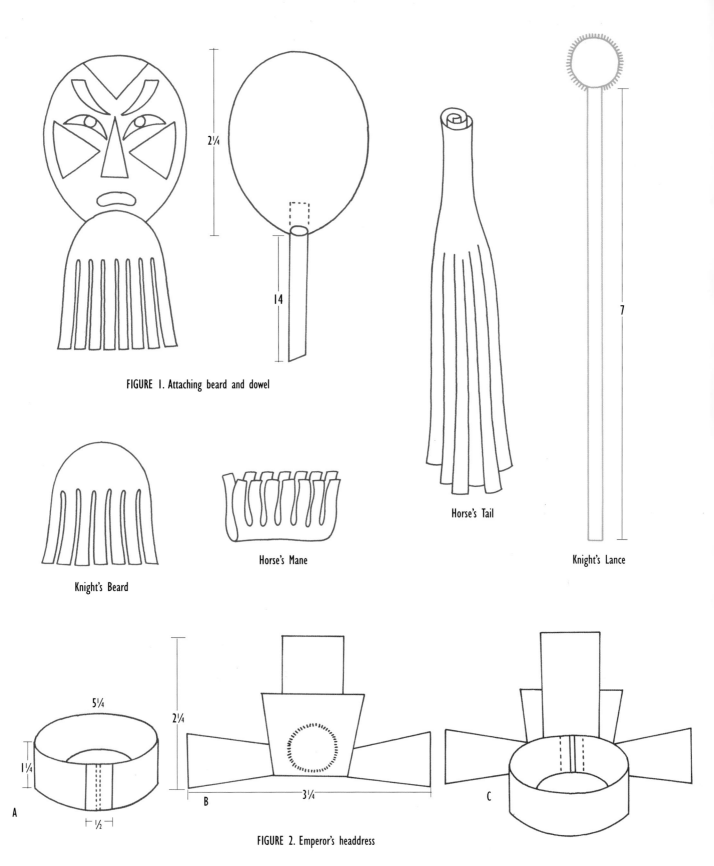

FIGURE 1. Attaching beard and dowel

Knight's Beard

Horse's Mane

Horse's Tail

Knight's Lance

FIGURE 2. Emperor's headdress

Headddress

1½

1¼

3

5¾

2

5½

The Knight

Headdress

Beard

7½

1¾

6¼

4

The Emperor

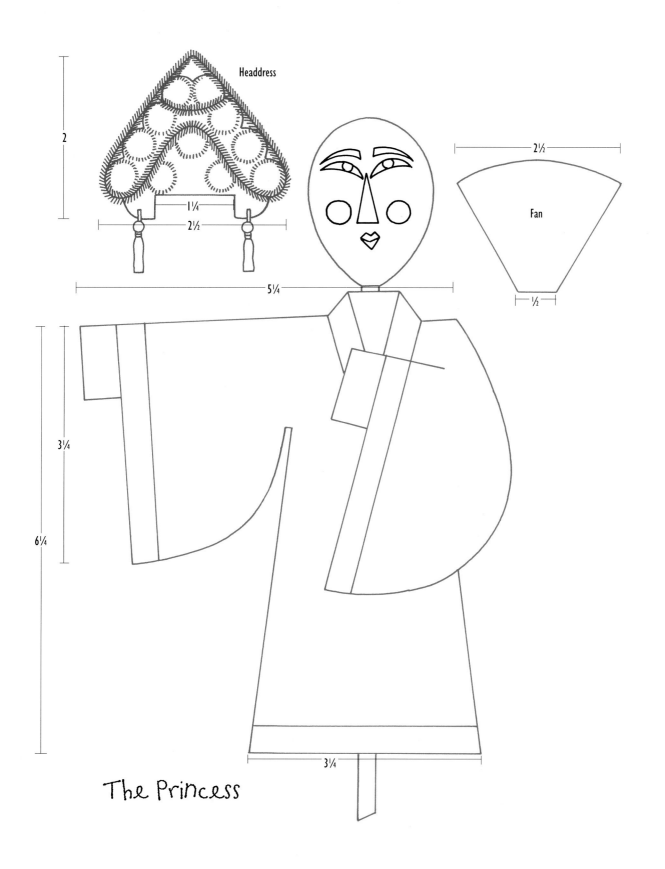

Headddress

2

1¼

2½

5¼

2½

Fan

½

3¼

6¼

3¼

The Princess

Headddress

Beard

2

1 ¼

2 ¾

5 ¼

2

6

4

The Executioner

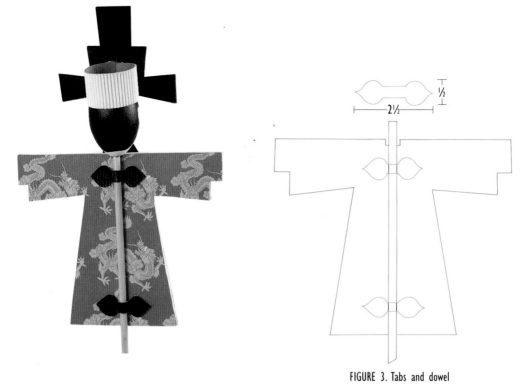

FIGURE 3. Tabs and dowel

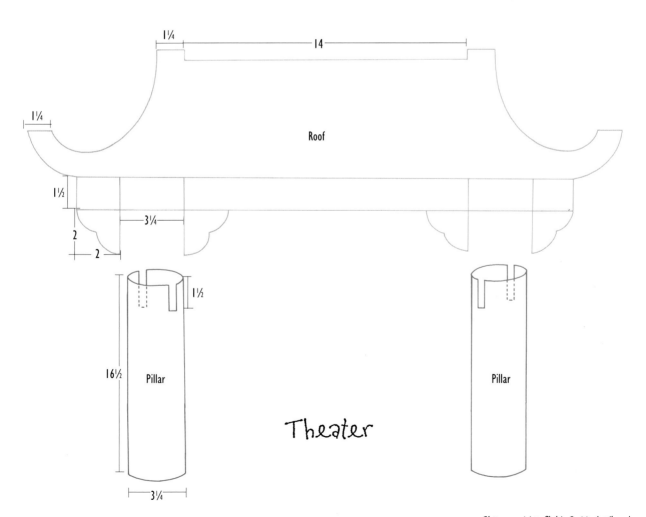

Roof

Pillar

Pillar

Theater

India

Darjeeling Toy Train

Two Fine Storytellers

"All aboard!" the conductor shouted.

"Toot! Toot!" The engine let out a big puff of steam. Slowly the Toy Train pulled out of Siliguri station and began to climb toward Darjeeling, a town high up in the Himalayan Mountains.

Gopi was on his way to visit his aunt in Darjeeling. Beside him a man with a big, bushy moustache sat writing in a large brown notebook. Gopi was curious. "What are you writing, sir?"

"I am writing a book about my travels," the bushy moustache man answered. "Maybe you can help me."

Gopi's eyes got big. How could a little boy help a man write a book? He felt he had to tell the man the truth. "Sir, I'm sorry to tell you I don't know anything at all about writing books."

"What can you tell me about where you live?" the man asked him.

"Oh, I can tell you a lot about that," Gopi assured him. And he told the man story after story about white elephants, princely peacocks, and holy cows. As he talked, the little train huffed and puffed up the mountain, twisted in and out of ravines, and rolled past villages and tea plantations.

When the train pulled into Darjeeling station, the man had filled the brown notebook with writing.

"That was wildly interesting and enchanting!" the man said to Gopi. "You have been very helpful to me in writing my book."

"But all I did was tell you stories," Gopi said. "Anyone could do that."

"No," said the man. "It takes a special kind of imagination to tell a good story." Then he reached into his bag and took out a book. As he held the book out to Gopi, he said, "I hope you'll enjoy this story I wrote as much as I enjoyed yours."

Gopi opened the book and read the first page. "The Adventures of Huckleberry Finn by Mark Twain." He tucked the book into his own satchel and followed the man off the train. On the platform, his aunt threw her arms around him and started talking so fast, he was afraid she would use up all the air in the station. "Gopi! Did you see that man with the big, bushy moustache? Did you happen to see him on the train? Gopi, that's the famous American writer Mark Twain! Come on, Gopi, hurry up! Stop interrupting! Whatever you have to tell me can't be as important as speaking to Mark Twain." So Gopi gave up trying to tell her about helping Mr. Twain write a book. He would tell her later.

Tale Tidbits

▶ Officially known as the Darjeeling-Himalayan Railway, the Darjeeling-Himalayan train is often called "the Toy Train" because of its narrow gauge of only two feet (60 centimeters). It runs from the town of Siliguri, at sea level, to Darjeeling, at nearly 7,000 feet (2 kilometers). The train takes more than seven hours to cover the 51 miles (81 kilometers) between the two towns.

▶ Author Samuel Clemens, whose pen name was Mark Twain, traveled on the Darjeeling-Himalayan train when he visited India in 1896.

▶ The Darjeeling Toy Train was inspired by the Darjeeling-Himalayan train and some of the animals of India. Three animals make up the train: an elephant, a white cow, and a peacock.

How to Make the Darjeeling Toy Train

MATERIALS

▶ Cardboard tubes, 1, 1¼, 1¾, and 3¼ inches in diameter

▶ 2 ply cardboard

▶ Clips and rubber bands

▶ Wood glue

▶ Tracing paper

▶ Fine, medium, and coarse sandpaper

▶ 13 tie-rack knobs

▶ 3 pieces of wood, 1 x 1 x 8½ inches, 1 x 1 x 6½ inches, and 1 x 1 x 4½ inches

▶ Wooden dowels, ³⁄₁₆ and ¼ inch in diameter

▶ 10 wooden washers, ¾ inch in diameter

▶ Corrugated paper

▶ White acrylic gesso

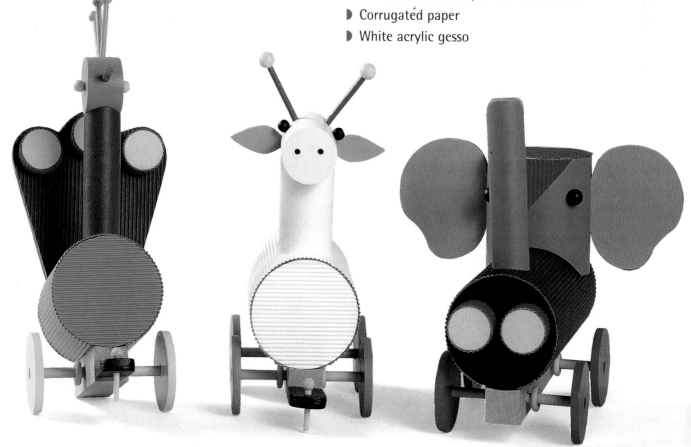

- Acrylic paints in desired colors
- 18 inches of string
- 2 wooden balls, ½ inch in diameter

TOOLS

- Pencil
- Steel ruler
- Cutting knife
- Scissors
- Handsaw
- Electric hand drill with ³⁄₁₆, ¼, and ³⁄₈-inch bits
- Paintbrushes

Before you begin: Be sure to read the General Instructions, pages 8–10.

STOKING THE ENGINE

BODY AND HEADLIGHTS (RED)

1. Cut an 8-inch piece of 3¼-inch tube. Cut a hole 1 inch in diameter on the top for the trunk/steam pipe. One-half inch from each end, drill a ¼-inch hole in the bottom of the tube.
2. Cut two round 3¼-inch lids from 4-ply cardboard.
3. Drill a ³⁄₁₆-inch hole near the edge of one lid for the tail, and glue on the other lid to close the front end of the tube. (Do not glue on the rear lid yet.)

4. Cut two ¾-inch pieces of 1¼-inch tube for the headlights.
5. Cut two round 1¼-inch lids from 2-ply cardboard, and glue a lid on one end of each piece.
6. Trace the outlines of the headlights on the front lid of the body.

HEAD, HEADDRESS, EARS, EYES, AND TRUNK (BLUE)

1. Cut a 3¾-inch piece of 3¼-inch tube and sand one end to shape it to fit the curve of the body. Cut two slits for the ears, each ³⁄₁₆ x 1¾ inches. Drill two ³⁄₁₆-inch holes for the eyes (see fig. 1).
2. Cut a round 4-ply lid 3¼ inches in diameter, and glue it on to close the top of the head.
3. Trace the outline of the head on the body.
4. For the headdress, cut two triangles from 3¼-inch tube.
5. Cut the two ears from 4-ply cardboard.
6. Cut part of the stem from two tie-rack knobs to make eyes.
7. Cut a 7-inch piece of 1-inch tube, and cut a V-shape in one end.

UNDERCARRIAGE AND HITCH (GREEN)

1. In the 1 x 1 x 8½-inch piece of wood, ¾ inch from each end, drill a hole ¼ inch in diameter and ½ inch deep. This is the top of the piece.
2. On one side, 1¼ inches from each end, drill horizontal ⅜-inch holes all the way through.
3. Drill one ³⁄₁₆-inch hole in the back end, ½ inch deep, ⅛ inch from the top.
4. With sandpaper, shape the top of the wood to fit the curve of the body.
5. Cut two 2½-inch pieces of ¼-inch dowel, and glue them in the ¼-inch holes in the top of the undercarriage. Then push the dowels into the ¼-inch holes in the body, and trace the outline of the undercarriage on the body.
6. For the hitch, cut a 1 x 1½-inch piece from 8-ply cardboard, and drill a ³⁄₁₆-inch hole in one end, ½-inch deep. Drill a ¼-inch hole through the piece, ⅜ inch from the other end.
7. Glue a 1-inch piece of ³⁄₁₆-inch dowel in the ³⁄₁₆-inch hole.

WHEELS (ORANGE)

1. Cut four 2½-inch wheels from 6-ply cardboard, and drill a ¼-inch hole through the center of each.
2. Cut two 4½-inch pieces of ¼-inch dowel.
3. Drill ¼-inch holes in four washers.

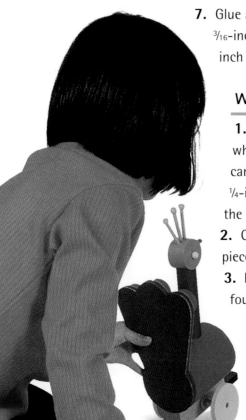

PAINTING AND CORRUGATING

1. Corrugate the back lid of the body and the front lid except the outlined headlight areas.
2. Corrugate the body except the outlined areas for the head and undercarriage.
3. Paint the head, then corrugate the top of the head.
4. Paint the edges of the headdress pieces, then corrugate them on one side.
5. Paint the edges and one side of the ears. Corrugate the backs of the ears except the ends that will be inserted in the head slits.
6. Paint the eyes, trunk, connector, and wheels.
7. Paint the headlight lids and corrugate them.

ASSEMBLING THE ELEPHANT ENGINE

1. Glue a washer over the hole in the back lid of the body. Put a string through the hole and knot it, leaving 4 inches hanging free outside the lid for a tail (red). Knot the string again 2 inches outside the lid.
2. Drill a ³⁄₁₆-inch hole through one of the wooden balls. Slide the ball on the string up to the knot, then tie another knot to secure it.
3. Glue, in this order: the back lid on the body, the ears and eyes in the head, the headdress pieces on the head, the head on the body.
4. Slide the trunk in the body and glue it, leaving 4¾ inches of trunk above the body.
5. Glue, in this order: the headlights to the front of the body, the connector to the rear of the undercarriage, the undercarriage to the body.

6. Slide the two ¼-inch dowels through the holes in the undercarriage, and glue two washers on each dowel, one on each side, ¼ inch from the undercarriage, so the wheels can turn freely (see fig. 2). Glue the wheels on the ends of the dowels.

GETTING THE COW CAR ROLLING
BODY AND HUMP (PURPLE)

1. Cut a 6-inch piece of 3¼-inch tube. Cut a 1¾-inch hole in the top for the neck and a ³⁄₁₆ x 1½-inch slit for the hump.
2. At each end, drill a ¼-inch hole in the bottom of the tube ½ inch from the edge.
3. Make two round 3¼-inch lids from 4-ply cardboard. Drill a ³⁄₁₆-inch hole near the edge of one lid and glue on the other lid to close the front of the tube. (Do not glue on the rear lid yet.)
4. Cut a hump from 4-ply cardboard.

HEAD, EARS, EYES, HORNS, AND NECK (PINK)

1. Cut a 2¼-inch piece of 1¾-inch tube for the head. Cut two ³⁄₁₆ x ¼-inch slits for ears.
2. Drill two ³⁄₁₆-inch holes for eyes and two ³⁄₁₆-inch holes for horns.
3. Make two round 1¾-inch lids from 4-ply cardboard. Drill two ³⁄₁₆-inch holes in one lid for nose holes, and glue on the lid to close the front of the head tube. Glue on the back lid.
4. Cut two 4-ply ears.
5. Cut part of the stem off two tie-rack knobs to make the eyes. Set aside two tie-rack knobs for horns.
6. Cut a 5-inch piece of 1¾-inch tube for the neck, and shape one end to fit the curve of the head.

Follow the instructions for the elephant, using the 1 x 1 x 6 ½-inch piece of wood. Instead of one hitch, make two. Attach one to the front end of the undercarriage (in the lower half) and the other to the back end (in the top half).

PAINTING AND CORRUGATING

1. Corrugate the front and back lids of the body. Corrugate the body except the outlined area for the undercarriage.
2. Paint the head except the area that will be glued to the neck.
3. Paint the eyes. Paint the edges and one side of the ears. Corrugate the backs of the ears.

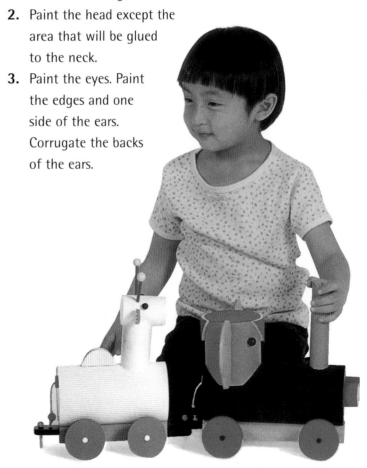

4. Paint the horns, neck, and the edge of the hump. Corrugate the hump except the end that will be inserted into the slit.

5. Paint the hitches and wheels.

ASSEMBLING THE COW CAR

1. For the string tail, follow the directions for assembling the elephant (steps 1 and 2).

2. Glue the ears, eyes, and horns in the head and the head to the neck.

3. Slide the neck into the body and glue it at an angle, leaving 3 inches above the body.

4. Glue the hump in the body and the undercarriage to the body.

5. Attach the wheels as for the elephant.

HOOKING UP THE PEACOCK CABOOSE

BODY AND TAIL (LIME)

1. Cut a 4-inch piece of 3¼-inch tube, and cut a 1-inch hole in the top for the neck.

2. At each end, drill a ¼-inch hole in the bottom of the tube ½ inch from the edge.

3. Make one round 3¼-inch lid from 4-ply cardboard, then glue it on to close the front.

4. Cut the tail from 6-ply cardboard.

5. Cut three ½-inch pieces of 1¼-inch tube for the eyes of the tail. Make three round 1¼-inch lids from 2-ply cardboard, then glue one on one side of each eye tube.

6. On the tail, trace the outline of the eyes and of the body.

HEAD, CROWN, BEAK, EYES, AND NECK (LAVENDER)

1. Cut a ¾-inch piece of 1¾-inch tube. Drill three ³⁄₁₆-inch holes for the crown and one ³⁄₁₆-inch hole for the beak.

2. Make two round 1¾-inch lids from 4-ply cardboard, and drill a ³⁄₁₆-inch hole through the center of each. Glue on the lids to close the head tube.

3. Cut off part of the stems of two tie-rack knobs to make the eyes. Set aside three tie-rack knobs for the crown.

4. For the beak, cut a 1-inch piece of ³⁄₁₆-inch dowel.

5. Cut a 6-inch piece of 1-inch tube for the neck, and shape one end of the tube to fit the curve of the head.

UNDERCARRIAGE, HITCH, AND WHEELS (GREEN AND ORANGE)

Follow the instructions for the elephant, using the 1 x 1 x 4½-inch piece of wood. Instead of four wheels, the peacock has two: Drill a ⅜-inch hole through the center of the side of the undercarriage. The peacock has one hitch on the bottom half of the front end of the undercarriage.

PAINTING AND CORRUGATING

1. Corrugate the front of the body and the body except the outlined area for the undercarriage.
2. Paint the edge of tail, and corrugate the tail on both sides except the outlined areas for the body and eyes of the tail.
3. Paint the lids of the three tail eyes, and corrugate the tubes.

4. Paint the head except where the neck will be glued. Paint the crown, eyes, beak, neck, connector, and wheels.

ASSEMBLING THE PEACOCK CABOOSE

1. Glue, in this order: the eyes to the tail, the tail to the body, the crown, eyes, and beak in the holes in the head, the head on the neck.
2. Slide the neck through the hole in the body and glue it, leaving 4 inches of neck above the body.
3. Glue the undercarriage to the body and the hitch to the undercarriage.
4. Attach the wheels as for the elephant.

ASSEMBLING THE DARJEELING TOY TRAIN

To connect the elephant, the cow, and the peacock, slide tie rack knobs through the hitches.

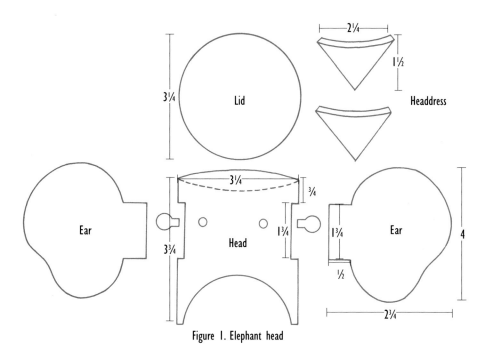

Figure 1. Elephant head

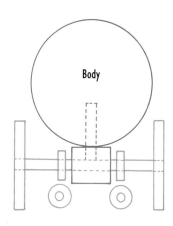

Figure 2. Front view of undercarriage

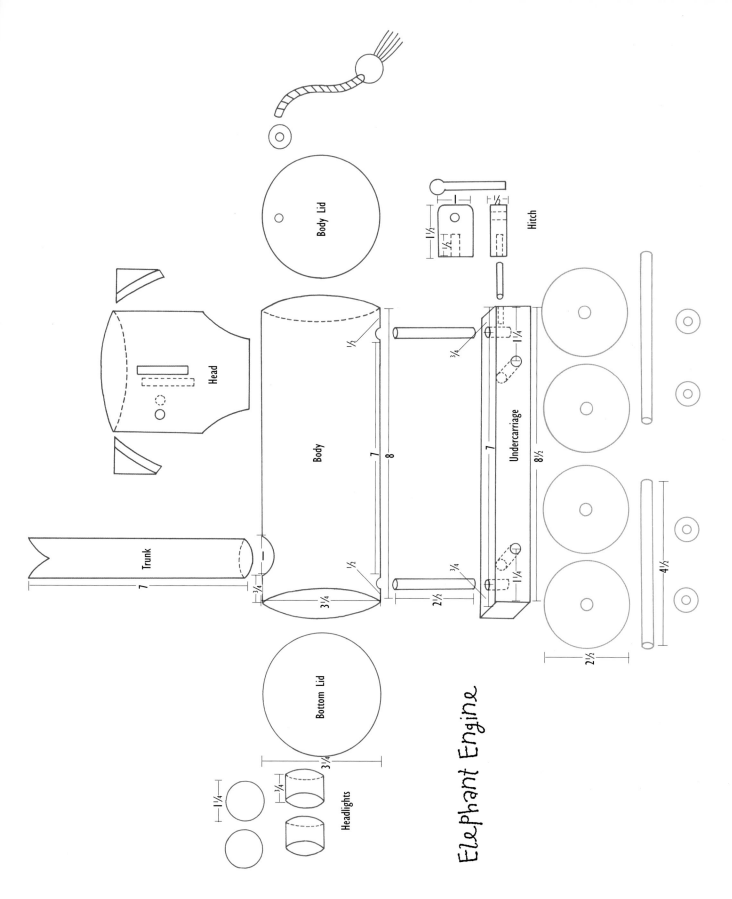

Body Lid

Hitch

1½

½

Head

Body

½

7

8

Trunk

7

¾

3/4

½

½

3/4

3/4

2½

7

Undercarriage

8½

1¼

1¼

4½

2½

Bottom Lid

3/4

1¼

3/4

Headlights

Elephant Engine

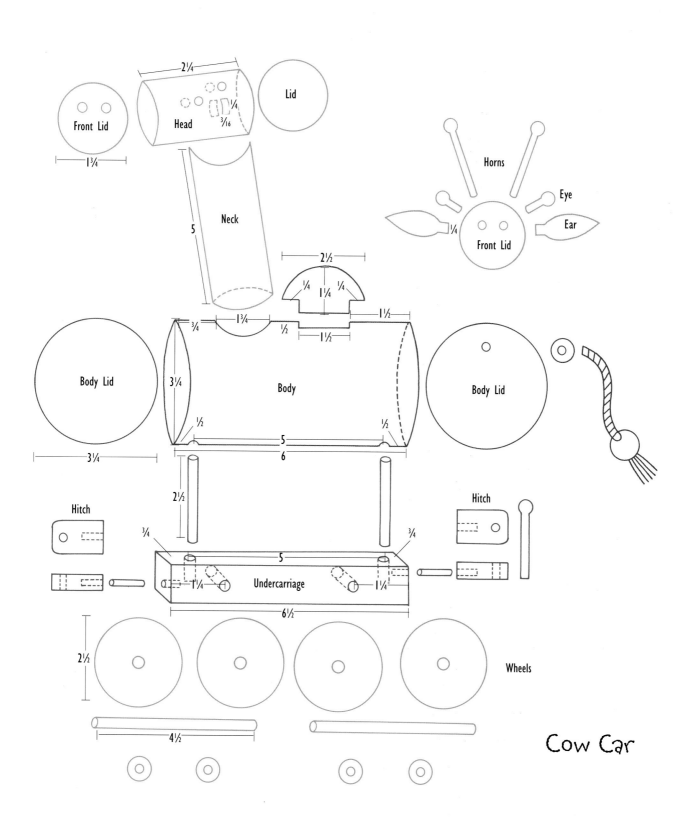

Front Lid

2¼

Head ¼ ³⁄₁₆

Lid

1¾

Horns

Eye

Ear

Front Lid ¼

Neck 5

2½

¼ 1¼ ¼

3¾

1¾ ½

1½

1½

Body Lid

3¼

Body

Body Lid

½ 5 ½

6

3¼

2½

Hitch

Hitch

¾

¾

Undercarriage

1¼ 5 1¼

6½

2½

Wheels

4½

Cow Car

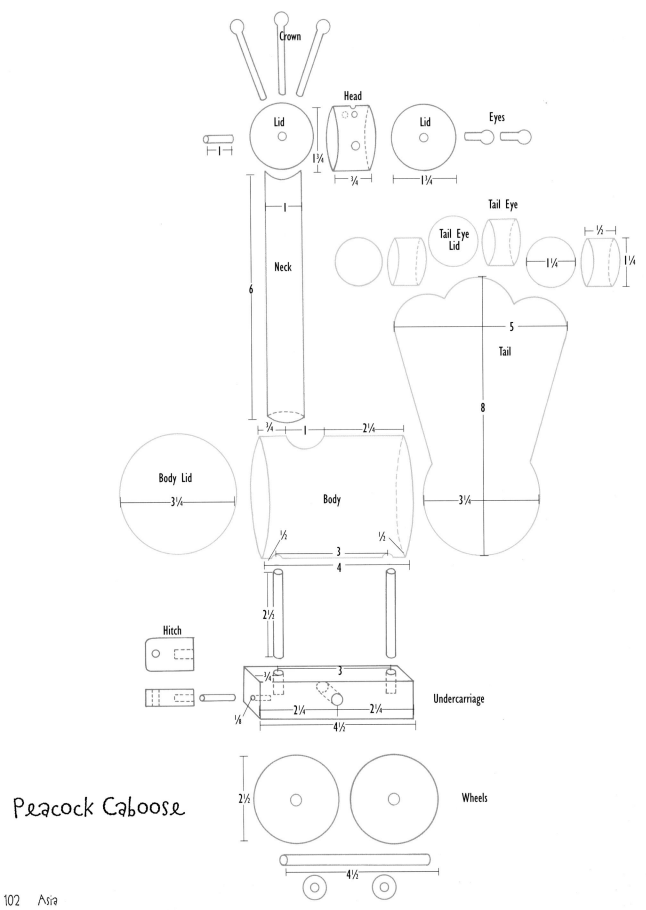

Crown

Head

Lid

Lid

Eyes

1¾

¾

1¾

Neck

1

6

Tail Eye

Tail Eye
Lid

½

1¼

1¼

Tail

5

8

¾ 1 2¼

Body Lid

Body

3¼

3¼

½ ½

3

4

2½

Hitch

3

¾

Undercarriage

1/8

2¼

2¼

4½

Wheels

2½

Peacock Caboose

4½

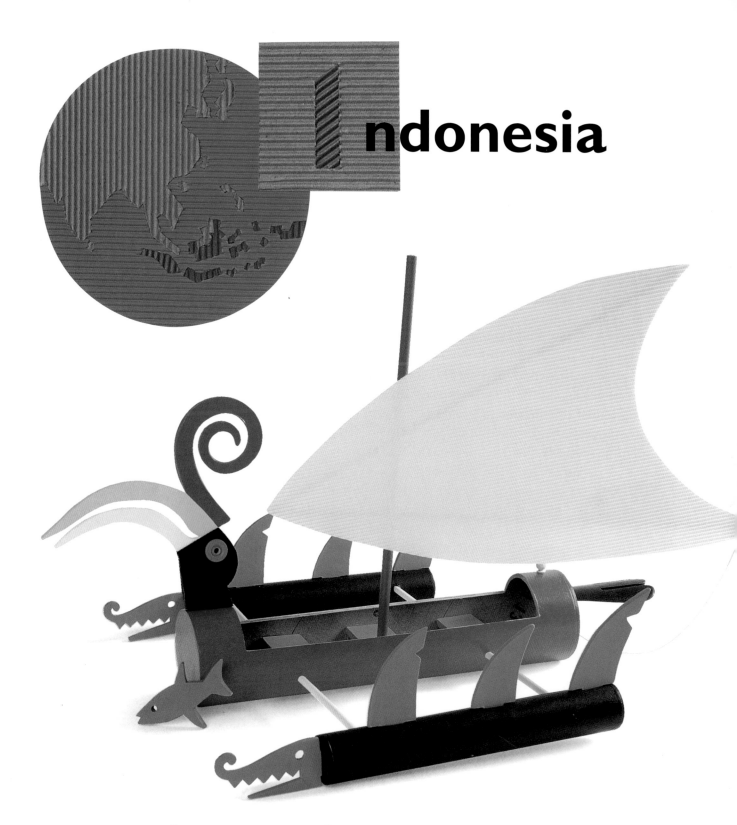

Indonesia

Hornbill Outrigger

The Hornbill Outrigger and the North Star

Chepaka lived on a tiny tropical island in northern Indonesia. Every night he looked at the sky and marveled at the bright, twinkling star that had guided the sailors of his island since the beginning of time.

One night as he watched, the star streaked across the sky like a comet and fell into the dark sea.

How would the sailors of the village find their way home? He ran to his small outrigger canoe, pushed it into the water, and sailed out to sea. The outrigger flew over the waves, its sail full of wind. The great hornbill on the prow pointed the way. He knew he must hurry, or all the sailors would be lost.

When Chepaka reached the place where the twinkling star had fallen, he jumped into the water and swam to the bottom of the sea to look for it. He searched and searched. No star. He came up for air and dove down again. This time he found the star. No wonder he hadn't found it the first time—it no longer twinkled.

Chepaka sailed his outrigger home, the star sitting safe in the bottom of the boat. He pulled the boat onto the beach. Now he was very tired. Hurry! he told himself. Think of the sailors! He lifted the fallen star from his canoe and carried it home. There he warmed it by the fire. But the warm fire made Chapaka sleepy. I'll just shut my eyes for a minute, he thought. But he went right to sleep, sailors or no sailors.

Soon the little star started to glow. Brighter and brighter it grew, twinkling and shimmering so brightly that it woke Chepaka up. He carried the star outside, where he was relieved to see it was still dark. Once again he climbed into his hornbill outrigger and placed the star carefully in the bottom of the boat. Once again they flew over the waves, the hornbill pointing the way, back to the spot where the star had fallen. Chepaka held the star up as high as he could, and the star streaked across the sky like a comet, back to its home.

It was nearly morning when the sailors of the village returned home, just as they did every night.

But Chepaka knew this night was not just like every night. He looked up at the North Star shining brightly in the sky and smiled.

Tale Tidbits

▶ The hornbill is a species of great-billed birds found in Indonesia.

▶ In ancient times, sailors navigated by the stars at night.

▶ The Hornbill Outrigger is based on the double outrigger canoe found throughout Southeast Asia and the Pacific.

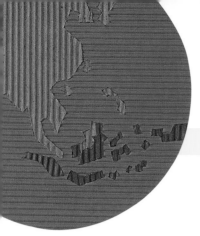

How to Make a Hornbill Outrigger

MATERIALS

- Cardboard tubes, 1½ and 3¼ inches in diameter
- 2-ply cardboard
- Clips and rubber bands
- Wood glue
- Wooden dowels, ³⁄₁₆, ¼, and ³⁄₈ inches in diameter
- 15 inches of string
- White corrugated paper
- Fine, medium, and coarse sandpaper
- Wooden washer, 1 inch in diameter
- White acrylic gesso
- Acrylic paints in desired colors
- 2 wooden washers, ¾ inch in diameter
- One tie-rack knob
- Tracing paper
- Corrugated paper

TOOLS

- Pencil
- Steel ruler
- Cutting knife
- Scissors
- Handsaw
- Electric hand drill with ¹⁄₁₆, ³⁄₁₆, ¼, and ³⁄₈-inch bits
- Paintbrushes

Before you begin: Be sure to read the General Instructions, pages 8–10.

LAUNCHING THE OUTRIGGER

HULL, HEAD, AND TAIL (RED)

1. Cut a 14-inch piece of 3¼-inch tube and cut out an 11 x 3-inch rectangle, leaving 1½ inches of hull at each end.

2. Drill two horizontal ¼-inch holes all the way through the tube, 2⅝ inches from the top of the hull and 3⅝ inches from each end. (The holes will be 6¾ inches apart.)

3. Cut a ¼ x 1-inch slit in the top front of the hull for the hornbill, and drill a ³⁄₁₆-inch hole in the top rear for the knob.

4. Make two round 3¼-inch lids from 4-ply cardboard, and make a ⅛ x ⅝-inch slit in one lid for the tail. Glue that lid to the back of the tube and the other lid to the front.

5. Cut out a hornbill head from 6-ply cardboard.

6. Cut the bird's tail from 3¼-inch tube.

MAST AND SAIL (BLUE)

1. Cut a 14¾-inch piece of ⅜-inch dowel for the mast.
2. Cut two 17-inch pieces of ³⁄₁₆-inch dowel. Drill a ¹⁄₁₆-inch hole through the end of one ³⁄₁₆-inch dowel to attach the string. Sand the side of the other end to fit the curve of the second dowel.
3. Cut two grooves at an angle in the mast, ³⁄₁₆ inch deep (see fig. 1).
4. Fit the ³⁄₁₆-inch dowels in the mast grooves, glue the dowel ends together, and glue the dowels in the grooves. Pull the string through the hole in the lower dowel and knot it.
5. Draw the sail on white corrugated paper and cut it out, then glue it to the mast.

BENCHES AND MAST BASE (LIME AND ORANGE)

1. Cut three 4-ply, 3 x 1½-inch pieces for the benches (lime).
2. Drill a ⅜-inch hole through the center of one bench, and adjust it to fit the mast.
3. With sandpaper, shape the edges of the benches to fit the curve of the hull.
4. Cut a 1½-inch piece of 3¼-inch tube for the mast base (orange).
5. Draw a vertical line on the tube, then measure 3⅞ inches around the tube and draw another vertical line. Cut the tube along the lines.
6. Drill a ⅜-inch hole through the center of the piece, and glue the piece in the center of the

inside of the hull (see fig. 2). Drill a ⅜-inch hole in a 1-inch washer and adjust it to fit the mast, then glue the washer on the mast base.

OUTRIGGERS (PURPLE)

For each outrigger:

1. Cut a 9¾-inch piece of 1½-inch tube. Drill two ¼-inch holes through the tube, 1½ inches from the ends (6¾ inches apart). Cut three ³⁄₁₆ x ¾-inch slits in the top for the shark fins.
2. Make two round 1½-inch lids from 4-ply cardboard. Cut a ³⁄₁₆ x ¾-inch slit in one lid for the shark head, then glue on the lid to close the front of the tube. Glue on the other lid to close the back.
3. Cut a 19¼-inch piece of ¼-inch dowel.
4. Cut a shark head and three fins from 4-ply cardboard.

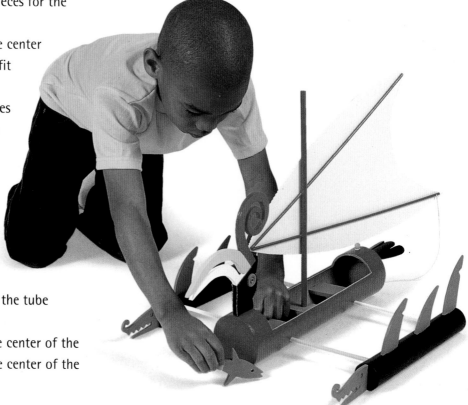

PAINTING AND CORRUGATING

1. Paint the hull and the edge of the hornbill. Corrugate the hornbill except the end that will go into the slit.
2. Glue ¾-inch washers on each side of the hornbill for eyes.
3. Paint the tail, benches, outriggers, shark heads and fins, and ¼-inch dowels.

ASSEMBLING THE HORNBILL OUTRIGGER

1. Glue, in this order: the hornbill head in the slit, the tail in the back lid, the shark heads in the front lids of the outriggers, the fins in the top slits of the outriggers.

2. Slide the dowels through the holes in the outriggers and the boat, then glue them in.
3. Glue the center bench in the hull, with the hole lined up with the washer in the mast base (see fig. 2). Glue in the other two benches above the dowels.
4. Cut part of the stem off the tie-rack knob, then glue the knob in the hole in the top back of the hull.
5. Insert the mast in the hole (fig. 2), and tie the string to the tie-rack knob.

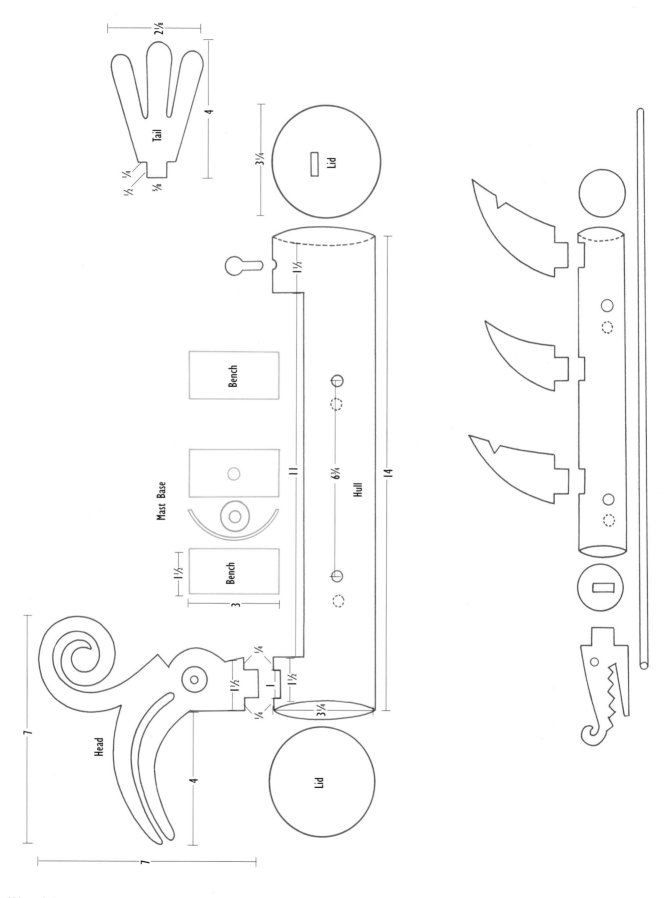

Tail

2⅛

¼

½ ⅝

4

Lid

3¾

1½

Bench

Mast Base

1½

Bench

3

11

6¾

14

Hull

¼

¼

1½

1½

1

¼

1½

3¼

Head

7

4

7

Lid

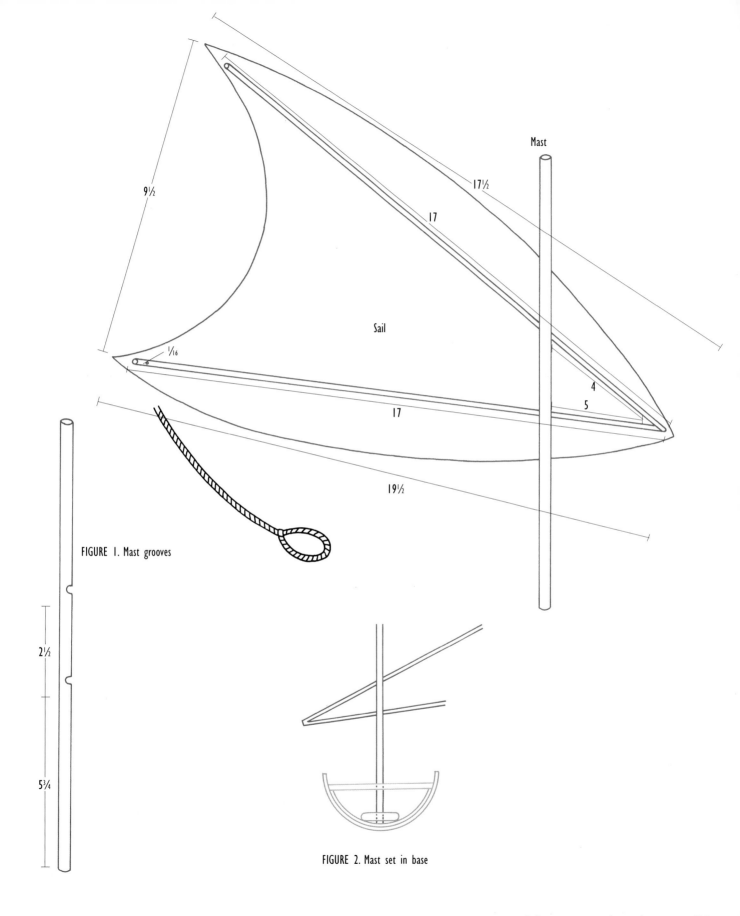

9½

Mast

17½

17

Sail

1/16

4

5

17

19½

FIGURE 1. Mast grooves

2½

5¾

FIGURE 2. Mast set in base

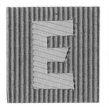

Solomon Islands

Hammerhead Sharkmobile

The Soapbox Car Race

All the villagers on the small island stood on a hill to watch a strange new race. An American soldier had told the village children about the soapbox car races back in his hometown in the United States. By now they had worked for many weeks to make cars from wooden crates, tin cans, and cardboard boxes left behind after the war. They were ready to have their own soapbox car race.

Four soapbox cars pulled up to the starting line—Stingray, Sawfish, Sea Moth, and Sharkmobile.

Sharkmobile had three tall back fins and a lot of fierce teeth. Each team had chosen its bravest member to drive its car.

The drivers walked proudly to their cars and climbed in. They reminded the older villagers of the days when island boys rode on the backs of sharks to honor the souls of the ancestors.

The drivers pulled on their coconut helmets for protection. Everyone watched the starter, who raised his arm high over his head. He waited until the only sound on the hill was the breeze blowing through the palm fronds.

"Go!" shouted the starter. A loud cheer went up as the cars started rolling down the hill, slowly at first, then faster and faster. The race was so close, some people thought it would be a four-way tie, and they thought that would be a good thing. Then every team would win.

But halfway down Stingray got stuck in the mud. Then Sawfish lost a wheel and tipped over.

Now the race was between Sea Moth and Sharkmobile. Near the bottom of the hill, with both cars racing fast as the wind, Sea Moth got thrown off course by a conch shell buried in the mud.

The driver of Sharkmobile raised his arms over his head as he rolled past the finish line first. "Just like the old days!" an old man shouted. "Just like the shark riders!"

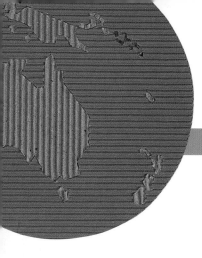

How to Make a Hammerhead Sharkmobile

MATERIALS

- Cardboard tube, 3¼ inches in diameter
- 2-ply cardboard
- Clips and rubber bands
- Fine, medium, and coarse sandpaper
- Wood glue
- 2 small tie-rack knobs
- White corrugated paper
- Wooden dowel, ¼ inch in diameter
- Tracing paper
- Corrugated paper
- White acrylic gesso
- Acrylic paints in desired colors
- 4 wooden washers, 1 inch in diameter

TOOLS

- Pencil
- Steel ruler
- Cutting knife
- Scissors
- Handsaw
- Electric hand drill with ¼ and ⁵⁄₁₆-inch bits
- Paintbrushes

Before you begin: Be sure to read the General Instructions, pages 8-10.

TUNING UP THE SHARKMOBILE

BODY AND FINS (BLUE AND RED)

1. Cut a 20¼-inch piece of 3¼-inch tube for the body (blue).
2. For the wheel openings, drill a pair of ⁵⁄₁₆-inch holes horizontally through the tube, 6 inches apart and 2½ inches from the top.
3. On the top of the tube, cut three slits for the top fins—for the tail fin and front fin, cut slits ¼ x 3 inches; for the middle fin, cut a slit ¼ x 2½ inches.
4. For the mouth, cut a 1½ x 3-inch horizontal slit at the front of the tube, leaving 1 inch above it for the top jaw and ¾ inch below for the bottom jaw.
5. For the hammerhead, cut a horizontal slit ¼ x 2 inches, ¼ inch from the top.

6. For the side fins, cut three slits horizontally all the way through the tube, 2½ inches from the top—for the two front fins, cut slits ¼ x 3 inches; for the back fin, cut a slit ¼ x 2¼ inches.

7. Cut two round 3¼-inch lids from 4-ply cardboard, and glue one to close the back end of the tube. Cut the other lid in three pieces to close the jaws and upper front of the tube (above the hammerhead slit), but do not glue them on.

8. For the inside back of the mouth, cut a 3-inch circle from 4-ply cardboard (red).

9. Cut three side fins, two top fins, and one tail fin from 6-ply cardboard (red).

HAMMERHEAD, EYES, AND TEETH/GUMS (GREEN)

1. Cut a hammerhead from 6-ply cardboard and cut a ³⁄₁₆-inch hole in each outside edge for the eyeholes.

2. Trim the stems of two tie-rack knobs to points to fit in the eyeholes.

3. Draw 23 teeth/ gums on white corrugated paper, 11 for the bottom jaw and 12 for the top, and cut them out.

WHEELS (ORANGE)

1. Cut four 1¼-inch pieces of 3¼-inch tube.

2. Cut eight round 3¼-inch lids from 4-ply cardboard, and drill a ¼-inch hole through the center of each. Glue on the lids to close both ends of each wheel tube.

3. Cut two 8-inch pieces of ¼-inch dowel.

PAINTING AND CORRUGATING

1. Paint the 3-inch lid for the inside of the mouth.

2. Corrugate, in this order: the back lid for the body, the three front-lid pieces, and the body.

3. Paint, in this order: the top and side fins, hammerhead, eyes, and the lids of the wheels.

4. Corrugate the wheel tubes.

5. Paint four 1-inch washers for the wheels.

ASSEMBLING THE SHARKMOBILE

1. Slide the three side fins through the slits in the sides of the body and the three top fins through the slits in the top of the body (see fig. 1).

2. Inside the mouth, glue the 3-inch lid against the front fin. Paint the inside of the mouth.

3. Glue on the three pieces of the front lid to the front of the body.

4. Glue the teeth in the mouth, with three teeth in the front of the bottom jaw and four teeth in the front of the top jaw (see figs. 2 and 3).

5. Slide the hammerhead in the slit above the top jaw, and glue the eyes in the holes in the hammerhead (see fig. 1).

6. Slide the two ¼-inch dowels through the holes in the body and wheels (see fig. 4). Glue the wheels to the dowels, leaving enough space between the wheels and the body so the wheels can turn. Glue the 1-inch washers on the ends of the dowels.

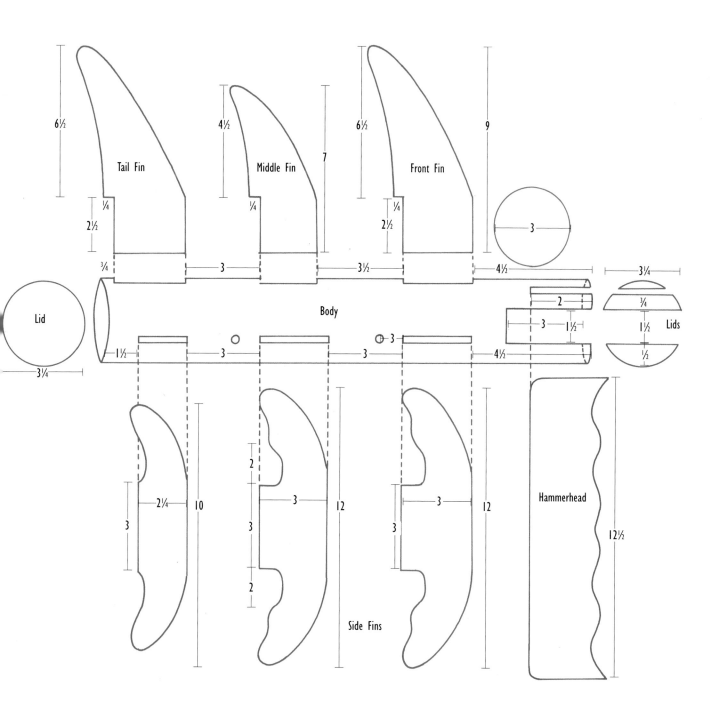

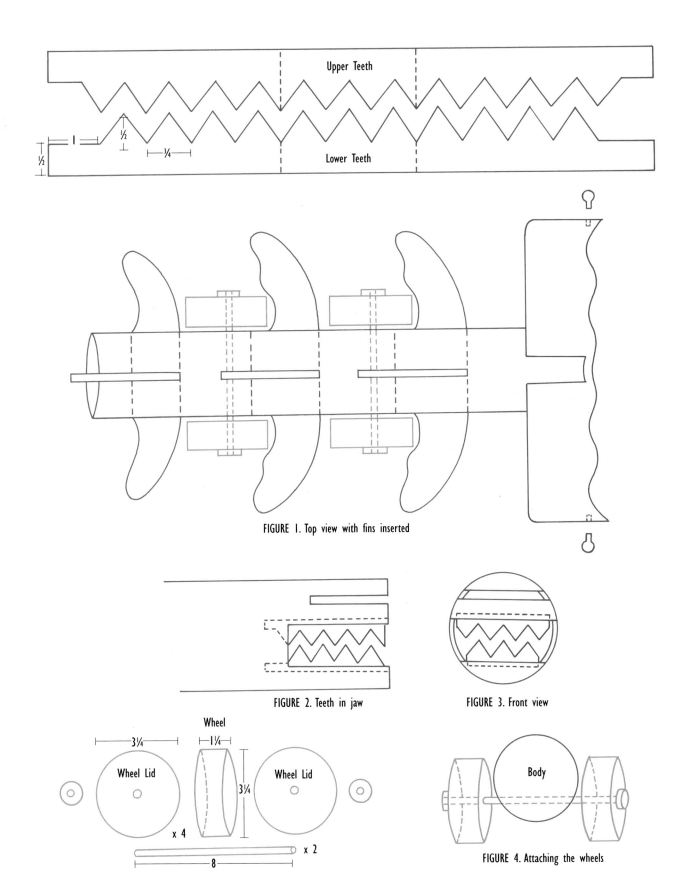

Upper Teeth

Lower Teeth

½
1
¾
½

FIGURE 1. Top view with fins inserted

FIGURE 2. Teeth in jaw

FIGURE 3. Front view

Wheel

Wheel Lid

3¼

1¼

3¼

Wheel Lid

x 4

8

x 2

Body

FIGURE 4. Attaching the wheels

Australia

Dreamtime Animals

Honey Ant

Kangaroos

Rainbow Snake

Red Roo and the Kangaroo Dance

When Red Roo was old enough, Mother Kangaroo took him on a walkabout to teach him about the land Rainbow Snake had made in the time of the Dreaming. She showed him the mountains and the bush and the deserts, the great waterfalls and rivers. She told him the secrets of the other animals—for instance, where Honey Ant kept his honey. She told him everything he needed to know to stay cool in the winter, warm in the cold months of summer, and healthy in the spring and fall.

That evening, Red Roo rested in his mother's pouch. The day had been long and full. He yawned, settling in for the night. Then a strange sound in the distance made him perk up his ears. First he stuck his head up out of the pouch, then he jumped out and hopped toward the sound, disappearing into the bush before his mother could catch him. "Red Roo! Come back!" she called. "It's too dark and too late for you to be hopping about!" But Red Roo kept going. He pretended not to hear.

As he came closer to the sound, Red Roo saw Old Man sitting by a fire playing a didgeridoo. Now that Red Roo could hear the music clearly, he caught its rhythm and started to hop around the fire. He jumped up and down and upside down to the sound of Old Man's music!

Old Man's eyes sparkled as he watched Red Roo dance. His foot started tapping. His head started bobbing. Before long he was jumping up and down and upside down too, hopping around the fire with Red Roo, dancing his Kangaroo Dance.

How to Make the Dreamtime Animals

MATERIALS FOR KANGAROOS

- Cardboard tubes, 1¾ and 3¼ inches in diameter
- 2-ply cardboard
- Clips and rubber bands
- Wood glue
- Fine, medium, and coarse sandpaper
- 4 small tie-rack knobs
- Wooden dowel, ¼-inch in diameter
- Tracing paper
- Corrugated paper
- White acrylic gesso
- Acrylic paint in desired colors
- 6 wooden washers, 1 inch in diameter

TOOLS

- Pencil
- Steel ruler
- Cutting knife
- Scissors
- Handsaw
- Electric hand drill with ³⁄₁₆, ¼, and ⁵⁄₁₆-inch bits
- Paintbrushes
- Hole puncher

Before you begin: Be sure to read the General Instructions, pages 8–10.

GETTING THE KANGAROOS HOPPING

MOTHER'S BODY AND HEAD (RED)

1. Cut a 4¾-inch piece of 3¼-inch tube, then drill two ⁵⁄₁₆-inch holes in it.
2. Cut two ¼ x ¾-inch slits for front paws and one ½ x 1-inch slit for the tail.
3. Make a round 3¼-inch lid from 4-ply cardboard, and cut a ¼ x 2¼-inch slit for the head. Glue on the lid to close the top of the tube.
4. Cut the head from 6- ply cardboard.
5. Drill two ³⁄₁₆-inch holes for eyes. Trim the stems off two tie-rack knobs for the eyes.

FRONT PAWS, LEGS, TAIL, AND POUCH (BLUE)

1. Cut two front paws, two legs, and a tail from 6-ply cardboard.
2. Drill ¼-inch holes through the legs and tail.
3. Cut a 5½-inch piece of ¼-inch dowel and set it aside.
4. Cut a 2-inch piece of 1¾-inch tube for the pouch, then cut the piece in half vertically and sand it to fit the curve of the body tube.
5. Make a round 1¾-inch lid from 4-ply cardboard, cut it in half, and sand the straight edge to fit the curve of the body. Glue it on to close one end of the pouch.

BABY KANGAROO (LIME)

1. Cut the head from 6-ply cardboard, and sand and shape it to fit in the pouch.
2. Drill two $\frac{3}{16}$-inch holes in the head for eyes. Trim the stems off two tie-rack knobs for eyes.
3. Trace the outline of the pouch and baby kangaroo on the mother's body.

PAINTING AND CORRUGATING

1. Corrugate the mother kangaroo's body (tube and lid) except the area outlined in the diagram. Make dots by hole punching corrugated paper, then glue them on.
2. Paint the mother kangaroo in this order: head, eyes, front paws, legs, and tail.
3. Paint two washers.
4. Corrugate the pouch.
5. Paint the baby kangaroo, then the baby's eyes.

ASSEMBLING THE KANGAROOS

1. Glue, in this order: mother kangaroo's head in slit, eyes in holes, front paws in slits.
2. Glue the eyes in the baby kangaroo's head, then glue the pouch and the baby kangaroo to the body.
3. Slide the 5½-inch dowel through the hole in the mother's body. Slide on one 1-inch washer, then the tail, then another 1-inch washer. Glue the tail between the two washers in the middle of the dowel, inside the body tube (see fig. 1).
4. On one side of the dowel outside the tube, slide on a 1-inch washer, then a leg, then a painted washer. Glue the leg on the dowel between the washers, leaving space between the washer and the tube for freedom of movement. On the other side of the dowel, slide on a washer and leg and the other painted washer, then set the kangaroo on a flat surface: Make sure that when the tail is touching the surface, the legs sit flat. Then glue on the second leg in the same way as the first (see fig. 1).

MATERIALS FOR THE HONEY ANT

▶ Cardboard tubes, 1¼, 2, and 3¼ inches in diameter
▶ Wood glue
▶ About ⅓ cup of rice
▶ 2 wooden dowels, ⅛ and $\frac{3}{16}$ inch in diameter
▶ 4 wooden balls, ½ inch in diameter
▶ 4 small tie-rack knobs
▶ 2-ply cardboard
▶ Fine, medium, and coarse sandpaper
▶ Clips and rubber bands
▶ Tracing paper
▶ Corrugated paper
▶ White acrylic gesso
▶ Acrylic paint in desired colors

TOOLS

▶ Pencil
▶ Steel ruler
▶ Cutting knife
▶ Scissors
▶ Handsaw
▶ Electric hand drill with ⅛ and $\frac{3}{16}$-inch bits
▶ Paintbrushes
▶ Hole puncher

Before you begin: Be sure to read the General Instructions, pages 8–10.

HATCHING THE HONEY ANT

HONEY POT, LEGS, AND FEET (ORANGE)

1. Cut a 1¾-inch piece of 3¼-inch tube, then drill a ³⁄₁₆-inch hole centered on it.
2. Cut two round 3¼-inch lids from 4-ply cardboard. Glue one lid on each side to close the tube.
3. Cut four 5-inch pieces of ³⁄₁₆-inch dowel for legs.
4. Drill a ³⁄₁₆-inch hole in each wooden ball, then glue the balls to the ends of the dowel pieces.

BODY (GREEN)

1. Cut a 1-inch piece of 2-inch tube. Drill two ³⁄₁₆-inch holes opposite each other for connectors.
2. Drill two pairs of ³⁄₁₆-inch holes in the bottom of the tube for inserting legs.
3. Cut two round 2-inch lids from 4-ply cardboard. Glue one lid on one side of the tube, fill the tube with rice, and glue the second lid on the other side to close the tube.

HEAD, EYES, AND ANTENNAS (PURPLE)

1. Cut a ½-inch piece of 1¼-inch tube, and drill a ³/₁₆-inch hole centered on it. Drill a pair of ⅛-inch holes for antennas.
2. Cut two round 1¼-inch lids from 4-ply cardboard, and drill a ³/₁₆-inch hole through the center of each. Glue one lid to each side to close the head tube.
3. Trim the stems off two tie-rack knobs for the eyes.
4. Cut two 2½-inch pieces of the ⅛-inch dowel.
5. Cut the stems off two knobs, drill a ⅛-inch hole in each knob, and glue the knobs to the ends of the dowel pieces.

PAINTING AND CORRUGATING

1. Corrugate the honey pot and the body.
2. Make dots from corrugated paper with a hole puncher and glue them on the honey pot.
3. Paint the legs and the sides of the head, then corrugate the head tube.
4. Paint the eyes and antennas.

ASSEMBLING THE HONEY ANT

1. Glue the eyes and antennas in the head.
2. Cut two 1-inch pieces of the larger dowel, then glue them in the holes to connect the head, body, and honey pot.
3. Slide the legs through the holes in the body, adjust them to achieve balance, and glue them in place.

MATERIALS FOR RAINBOW SNAKE

- Cardboard tubes, 1¼ and 1¾ inches in diameter
- 2-ply cardboard
- Clips and rubber bands
- Fine, medium, and coarse sandpaper
- Wooden dowel, ³⁄₁₆ inch in diameter
- 2 tie-rack knobs
- Acrylic white gesso
- Acrylic paint in desired colors
- Wood glue
- Tracing paper
- Corrugated paper
- String to connect snake pieces

TOOLS

- Pencil
- Steel ruler
- Cutting knife
- Scissors
- Handsaw
- Electric drill with a ³⁄₁₆-inch bit
- Paintbrushes
- Hole puncher

Before you begin: Be sure to read the General Instructions, pages 8–10.

HATCHING RAINBOW SNAKE
HEAD, TONGUE, AND EYES (PINK)

1. Cut a 1¼-inch piece of 1¾-inch tube, then drill two ³⁄₁₆-inch holes on opposite sides for eyes. Drill two ³⁄₁₆-inch holes for the tongue.
2. Cut two round 1¾-inch lids from 2-ply cardboard, and glue one lid on the top and one on the bottom to close the tube.
3. Cut two 1½-inch pieces of dowel for the forked tongue.
4. Trim the stems off two tie-rack knobs for the eyes.

BODY AND TAIL (LAVENDER)

1. From a 1¼-inch tube, cut one 1-inch piece for the tail and eight 2-inch pieces for the body segments.
2. Shape one end of one 2-inch piece to fit the curve of the head.
3. Cut 17 round 1¼-inch lids from 2-ply cardboard for the ends of the body and tail segments. Drill a ³⁄₁₆-inch hole through the center of 16 of the lids.

PAINTING AND CORRUGATING

1. Paint the head tube, then corrugate the top and bottom of the head.
2. Make dots from corrugated paper with a hole puncher, then glue them on top of the head.
3. Paint the tongue, eyes, and lids.

ASSEMBLING RAINBOW SNAKE

1. Glue the two tongue parts in the holes in the head and the eyes in their holes.
2. Glue the lid without the hole onto the 1-inch segment at the end of the tail.
3. Tie pairs of lids together with string.
4. Glue the lids on the body and tail segments to close the tubes, then corrugate the tubes.
5. Glue the head to the body.

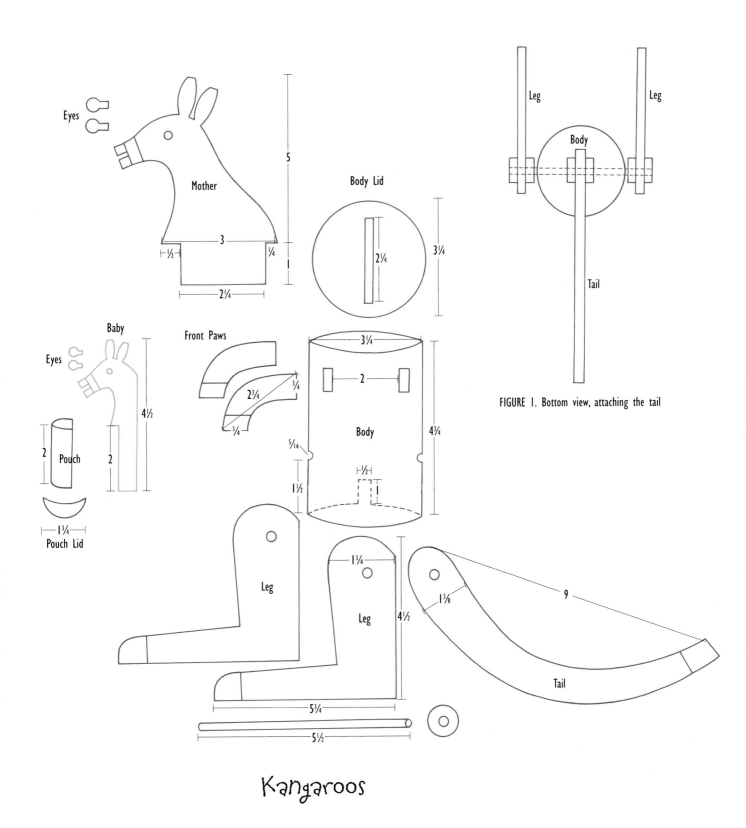

Eyes

Mother

5

3

½   ¼

1

2¼

Body Lid

2¼

3¼

Baby

Eyes

4½

Front Paws

2

Pouch

2¾

¾

¾

2

3¼

Body

2

4¾

5/16

1½

½

FIGURE 1. Bottom view, attaching the tail

Leg   Leg

Body

Tail

Pouch Lid

1¾

Leg

Leg

1¾

4½

1⅜

9

Tail

5¾

5½

Kangaroos

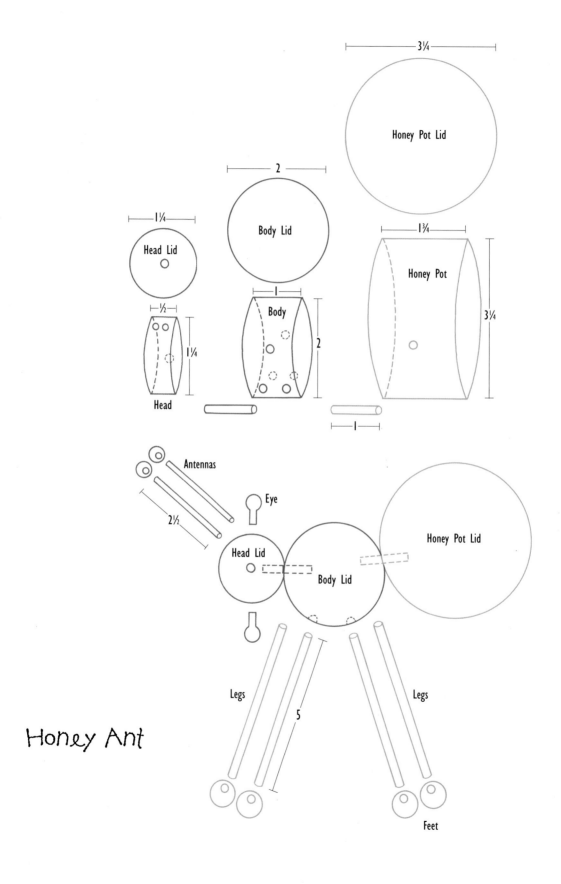

Honey Pot Lid — 3¼

Body Lid — 2

Head Lid — 1¼

Honey Pot — 1¾ / 3¼

Head — ½ / 1¼

Body — 1 / 2

1

Antennas

Eye

2½

Head Lid

Body Lid

Honey Pot Lid

Legs

Legs

5

Feet

Honey Ant

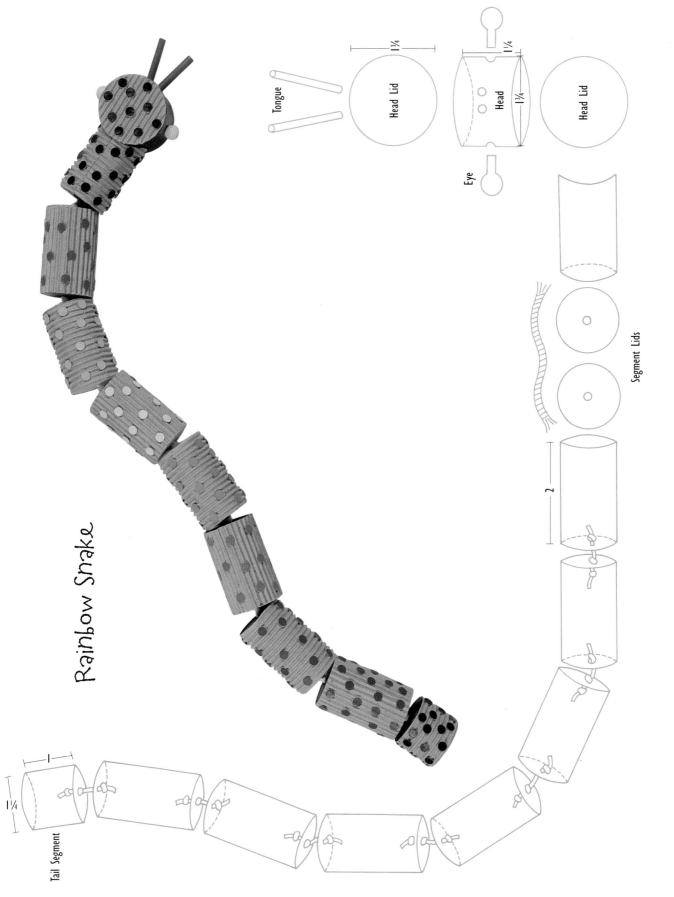

Rainbow Snake

Tongue

Head Lid

1¾

Head

1¼

1¾

Eye

Head Lid

Head Lid

Segment Lids

2

Tail Segment

1

1¼

Metric Conversion Chart

To convert inches to centimeters, multiply by 2.5 and round to the nearest tenth.

INCH	CM	INCH	CM	INCH	CM
1/16	.15	3	7.5	12	30
1/8	.3	3¼	8.1	13	32.5
3/16	.5	3½	8.8	14	35
¼	.6	3¾	9.4	15	37.5
5/16	.8	4	10	16	40
3/8	.9	4¼	10.6	17	42.5
7/16	1.1	4½	11.3	18	45
½	1.3	4¾	11.9	19	47.5
9/16	1.4	5	12.5	20	50
5/8	1.6	5¼	13	30	75
11/16	1.7	5½	13.8	33	82.5
¾	1.9	5¾	14.4	**CUPS**	**GRAMS**
13/16	2.0	6	15	⅓	60
7/8	2.2	6¼	15.6	1½	270
15/16	2.3	6½	16.3	2½	450
1	2.5	6¾	16.9		
1¼	3.1	7	17.5		
1⅜	3.5	7¼	18.1		
1½	3.8	7½	18.8		
1⅝	4.1	7¾	19		
1¾	4.4	8	20		
1⅞	4.7	8½	21.3		
2	5.0	9	22.5		
2¼	5.6	9½	23.8		
2½	6.3	10	25		
2¾	6.9	11	27.5		

About the Author

An award-winning writer and illustrator of 15 books for children, **Stefan Czernecki** lives in Vancouver, British Columbia. This book marks his fourth collaboration with **Michael Haijtink**, who lives in the Netherlands.